The author, Norman A. Katz, is a senior business and technology leader with a history of architecting and delivering best-in-class enterprise solutions for global companies that transform and strengthen the full spectrum of financial and supply chain operations. Norman accelerates profit and loss performance via technical and business process innovation. He collaborates with C-level leaders to introduce and adopt new ways of thinking and working, generating millions of dollars in top-line revenue performance. Norman is widely recognized in both technical and business circles for a proven ability to bridge complex business requirements with seamless, accessible solutions. He is a frequent presenter at global conferences on best practices and emerging trends.

Norman is a Lean Six Sigma Black Belt, a Certified Fraud Examiner, a Certified Controls Specialist, and a Microsoft Office specialist. Norman holds a Florida Private Investigator license, is a Florida notary public, and has a certification in corporate governance from Tulane University College of Law. Norman has a bachelor of science in business administration with a major in computer information sciences from the University of Florida.

Norman is the author of two first-of-their-kind exclusive books. *Detecting and Reducing Supply Chain Fraud* was published in August 2012. *Successful Supply*

Chain Vendor Compliance was published in December 2015. Aside from private sales, both books are available in hundreds of university libraries worldwide.

Norman began his professional career as a programmer and progressed to programmer analyst, business systems analyst, and information technology manager in the first eleven years after graduating from university and before starting his own advisory company, Katzscan Inc., in January 1996. He has experience in a variety of industries, notably consumer products within brick-and-mortar and online retail servicing both B2B and B2C fulfilment, pharmaceutical and medical products, and general manufacturing and distribution.

Norman began fencing in 1993 and started his own fencing club in 2007. He delights in teaching fencing to people of all ages and skill levels; a sport he truly loves participating in himself. Since he was a youngster, the thought of being a swordfighter was something he could only imagine while watching his heroes play out their fantastic fantasy roles on television and on the big screen. And now, every time he dons his fencing uniform, Norman gets to live out his childhood dreams, even way into adulthood; just one of the things, he surmises, that keeps him mentally, spiritually, and physically young. And what a fun time he has doing so!

For more information about Norman and his professional help to companies, please go to: www.katzscan.com

To Christin, who has made me – and continues to inspire me to – want to be better in everything I endeavor to do and accomplish.

Norman A. Katz

Attack, Parry, Riposte: A Fencer's Guide to Better Business Execution

AUSTIN MACAULEY PUBLISHERS™

LONDON · CAMBRIDGE · NEW YORK · SHARJAH

Ordering Information:
Quantity sales: special discounts are available on quantity purchases by corporations, associations, and others. For details, contact the publisher at the address below.

Publisher's Cataloging-in-Publication data
Katz, Norman A.
Attack, Parry, Riposte: A Fencer's Guide to Better Business Execution

ISBN 9781643789620 (Paperback)
ISBN 9781643789613 (Hardback)
ISBN 9781645365754 (ePub e-book)

Library of Congress Control Number: 2020908419

www.austinmacauley.com/us

First Published (2020)
Austin Macauley Publishers LLC
40 Wall Street, 28th Floor
New York, NY 10005
USA

mail-usa@austinmacauley.com
+1 (646) 5125767

I acknowledge that there are indeed circumstances when the pen is mightier than the sword, but it is not nearly as much darn fun.

Other Books by
Norman A. Katz

Detecting and Reducing Supply Chain Fraud
August 2012, Gower/Routledge, 258 pages,
ISBN: 9781409407324
For more information, go to:
www.supplychainfraud.com

Successful Supply Chain Vendor Compliance
December 2015, Gower/Routledge, 178 pages,
ISBN: 9781472472014
For more information, go to:
www.vendorcompliance.info

Table of Contents

About This Book

If business is a sport, I cannot conceive of a better comparison than to fencing. If, however, business is a battle, as it often is, and really truly is, there is likely no better one-on-one sport analogy that so well represents the competitive nature, analytical thinking, skillful use of weaponry (literal and figurative), comprehension of one's own and of the opponent's resources, and the individual discipline than that of fencing. Inasmuch as businesses are built on teams, these teams are structured upon individuals who are selected to lead them, create them, and comprise them. The qualities of a good fencer and a good team member are very much similar if a team is going to successfully drive execution and produce the desired output. As the saying goes, a team is only as strong as its weakest link. Individual strength is critical in ensuring teams are strong. Teams benefit from a variety of skills and perspectives. A fencer utilizes different senses (sight, sound, touch), employs critical thinking, relies upon their understood strengths, seizes upon their opponent's weaknesses, recognizes their own capabilities, knows when to get close and when to remain out of reach, must move at the speed of the competition, must be disciplined in approach, and has to be confident in ability.

I am both strategic and tactical in how I help companies improve their business execution from a combined software systems and operational viewpoint with a foundational ability to analyze their data and provide insights into their organization. I advise senior executives and mentor employee staff. (I have been asked if I am an "executive coach." I believe that there are certification courses for this designation. I have not taken any such accreditation nor do I hold a formal professional executive coaching credential. Nevertheless, I sometimes spend a significant amount of my time – at the company's request – dealing with personnel management issues.) I am a relationship champion, forging and building partnerships between internal and external stakeholders, such as between supplier/vendor companies and their top-level customers, between client companies and their supply chain partners like contract manufacturers and distributors, or between people from different operating departments.

As I became more involved and more experienced in coaching fencing, I came to realize the striking similarities between the lessons I was teaching my students and the software, operations, and management advice I was providing to companies. The principles between fencing and basic business were very uncannily similar. But this realization may be because I teach fencing the way I approach business problems: analytically and logically.

I instruct my fencing students in the moves and compound maneuvers used in fencing. I show them my legitimate little tricks, because my purpose is not to beat them but to make them be the best fencers they can be, and that includes getting them to be able to beat me if they can. However, it is not enough for my fencers to just mechanically mimic something I show them: they have to mentally understand the 'why' and 'how' of what they are doing. I break down the offensive and defensive maneuvers into their step-by-step moves. Every move and the counter-move options are reviewed and evaluated for their strengths and weaknesses, pros and cons. This includes each student's ability to execute the moves effectively or ineffectively given that each person has their own comfort level with different movements; the maneuvers students gravitate to the most become an inherent part of their repertoire and thus their unique style; other moves the student struggles with I will reinforce but not necessarily pressure upon them to use. My students have to become and 'be' a fencer, their own fencer, and they have to think like a fencer. This takes encouragement from the coach, patience from both the instructor and student, and time.

When I help companies, my task is to dig into their problems and discover the root causes of the issues. Whether I am performing data analysis, examining operational processes, interviewing people, or probing a software system for functionality concerns, the divide-and-conquer methodology of breaking down something larger into something smaller and then analyzing it step-by-step is the same. I pass along my knowledge to the company to make them better; I have no fear that they will become smarter than I am. In fact, I found it more than a little disingenuous that people asked me after I authored my prior two books if I wasn't afraid that people would just read my books and not hire me to help them, and whether I, therefore, held back information in the books. I stated that I wrote the books with the full expectation that they could be read and used on their own, without holding back any of my knowledge, but that sometimes a book alone is not enough and an expert will be needed to help. It is purely up to each individual person to decide.

Certainly, there are plenty of books about fencing, with videos about fencing freely available on the Internet. These are good places to start learning or discovery into something new. Yet people still recognize the value of paying for lessons from a professional or getting help from an expert because there is only so much knowledge and skill that can be acquired from a book or a video versus face-to-face, personal, or direct individual instruction or consultation.

This book is about taking the very applicable lessons learned from teaching fencing and highlighting their relationship to the world of business. Businesses small and large struggle unnecessarily to define their opponents – the opposing forces (which can be both internal and external) challenging them to execute better and successfully reach their goals – and to accurately target their problems, enabling them to fulfill their objectives. Fencing, as a strategic and analytical sport, provides what I believe every reader will find to be genuine parallels into the world of business. Owners, executives, leaders, and everyone involved in developing strategies and also those responsible for executing tactical procedures will discover insightful and relevant uses for this book in improving their own enterprises and organizations.

Because in business, it's best to be en garde.

Preface

I grew up watching creature-feature monster movies on the weekends, and I am still a rabid Godzilla fan to this day. The campiness of the movies does not bother me, in fact, it is one of the more endearing aspects. The miniaturization tricks used were good enough to wow me as a child and make me smile as an adult.

I also watched shows like the Kung Fu, The Lone Ranger, and Zorro, the latter of which was absolutely responsible for my intrigue in the sport of fencing. Heroes like these who had no mutant superpowers but instead relied upon their intellect, skills of strength, martial art moves, and weaponry technique mastery were of great fascination to me. Plus, let's be quite honest: swordsmanship is just plain cool.

As a youth, I recall wanting to take fencing lessons but was denied for reasons that have long since been obscured by time or were never made clear to me. Many years later when I was in university, the fencing classes offered always conflicted with my required courses and I never had the opportunity to try the sport much to my disappointment.

In 1992, I moved down to the South Florida area from North Carolina due to a change in jobs. I read the daily newspaper – something I still do today – and a year later I caught an article about local fencing clubs. I was excited! I contacted one of the clubs but just didn't like the person I spoke with: something about his attitude did not sit well with me. I contacted another one of the clubs mentioned in the article and really liked the person on the other end of the telephone, so that's the club I picked to investigate. I went the next week to check things out, subsequently joining on-the-spot and began my long and continuing love affair with the sport of fencing. I became a foil and sabre fencer, likely because those were the weapons fenced by my new-found troupe. I have tried epee on occasions but have never really gravitated to the weapon, though I will fence epee for the fun of it if someone puts one in my hand.

The club I originally belonged to merged, and then merged again and again, with other fencing clubs as the local clubs struggled to stay afloat. There was a period of about five years or so when I had no fencing club at all to call my own, as none existed anywhere nearby to me. Fortunately, a new club formed and I was able to return to fencing.

The new club was great and we even had a former Bulgarian Olympic and World Cup sabre fencer as a coach come in very frequently to instruct. We had a good club and kept things light and fun: it wasn't run in a rigid manner that was overly structured to the point of being a burden to be there. The club was renting a recreational space from a church, and I know that the club was not always running in the financial black, but the person who was managing the club because his son was involved was keeping the place fiscally going although I suspect he could ill-afford to do so.

At times, we had more fencers than our coach could handle, so as it is my nature, I jumped in to help and essentially became the assistant coach by default. My getting instructed from a former world-class fencer definitely helped me to sharpen my own skills. I was frustrated, however, because I noticed that my own progress had plateaued and I was not able to break through and figure out what I was doing wrong with some of my moves. It was not until I began coaching – analyzing what the students were doing, correcting their mistakes, and teaching them the skill sets – that I began to understand what I was doing wrong myself. The act of instructing, the external perspective and explanations I was providing to the students, was benefiting me by providing me the introspective perspective I needed to change what I was doing. And from that point, it didn't take too long for the improvements to my own fencing methods take hold.

I was also playing racquetball at that time and had seriously injured my right shoulder. (I am right-handed.) The injury was so severe that it would take several days after fencing for the pain to subside. My choices at the time were to stop fencing or to learn to fence left-handed and give my shoulder time to heal by itself. (I did not consider invasive surgery to be a practical option. Given that I was self-employed at the time, and still am at the time of my writing this book, the thought of being unable to work due to surgery was simply something I had to avoid.) Mentally and physically, I knew that learning to fence left-handed would be a challenge, but I really believed that I had no other choice. So, for three months I worked at teaching myself to fence left-handed, including practicing the opposite footwork at home, just like I practiced my original footwork when I was first learning to fence. Initially, every fencer, including every youngster, was beating me quite convincingly! Ugh! My confidence – as well as my fencing target area torso – was taking some serious figurative and literal hits during this time. However, after three months, I was completely ambidextrous, to the point where I would fence holding two swords and could shift my body mid-air, changing position from right-to-left or left-to-right handed against my opponent. (Granted, that is completely illegal in a competition, but people love watching me fence and do this!) And I still fence like this to this day. The benefit to my own students is that I can fence against them right-handed and left-handed, preparing them for whichever kind of opponent they are likely to face. For my students, they get a two-for-one coaching deal.

Regrettably, our coach parted from us one day, and very shortly afterward the location that we were renting decided to kick us and the other rental vendors out so they could repurpose the facility for other uses. With no leader and no home, the fencing club was on a path to closure. People were looking at me to take charge and take ownership, so I did in July 2007. I renamed the club Tropical Knights Fencing (www.tropicalknightsfencing.com) with a nod to our being located in sunny South Florida. Instead of paying rent which we could not afford, I found us a home at a city recreational facility where participants pay the city and the city simply takes a per attendee percentage of whatever the instructor decides to charge. This allows me to keep the fees very low, especially as some of our participating families are on extremely tight budgets. It is a good benefit for the city because fencing is a unique sport that attracts people to the facility where I instruct. The fencing club is my hobby, it is neither my business nor my primary source of income, though I do of course have to treat the club as a business and maintain insurance and market it through social media and maintain a supply of spare equipment for newcomers who want to give it a non-committal try. And while my club rarely breaks financially even each year after year, I don't mind covering the minor expenses of the club if it keeps me in fencing, makes the sport accessible to my local community, and keeps fencing available to my participants, some of whom have become valuable friends.

I have been running my own club since 2007. I am not a certified fencing coach. I hope the last sentence there does not disappoint any of you or discourage you from continuing to read this book or lose faith in me as a fencing coach. Certification is not required to be a coach, nor is the term 'coach' an official designation in regards to a fencing instruction certification ranking. The national fencing association itself does not credential instructors; this is done by another and disconnected group. The title of 'coach' was bestowed upon me by the father with the young fencer who ran the club before I took it over, and it has just stuck. Nonetheless, it accurately describes what I do in teaching the sport of fencing from what I consider to be a holistic (physical and intellectual) perspective as you will discover in this book.

While some fencing clubs in my area only want to engage with the superstars, and I have had parents bring their children to my club after being rejected by other local fencing clubs, I welcome all participants: anyone who wants to fence can find a welcome home at Tropical Knights Fencing. To the parents, I joke that the only way I am likely to take their child to the Olympics is if I drive them there myself. But if I believe that their child is a fencing prodigy and is beating the knickers off of all of us, I will let them know. My recommendation will then be to pull their child out of school; get a dedicated and credentialed fencing Master (probably from an Eastern European country) who will train their child eight hours each day, six days per week; get a tutor to continue their child's education; get ready to travel to fencing tournaments; have lots of money to support this new lifestyle. The parents just seem to smile as they realize that their child is not likely such a phenomenon, and I haven't had such a wonder-kid in my club yet. But I am always on the lookout.

I have had the pleasure of instructing many children and adults who have passed through my club. For the children, some of whom have learned to fence with me through their high school years, there have been those who have gone on to fence on their college or university club teams. Yes, that is correct: I have coached kids to be able to fence on their college and university club teams. I have also fenced with and coached world-class fencers who come to my club as part of their training regime. I have been asked to analyze their deficiencies and help them to improve some of their weaknesses. I helped a world champion overcome a deficiency she had in fencing a left-handed opponent by showing her how to counteract a particular left-handed attack: the benefits of my being ambidextrous, and I sure didn't need an instructing credential to analyze and resolve that problem. Through the years I have had students (children through adults) ages eight through 80, as all are welcome.

The fencing club business model is a little bit different than that of other types of martial arts studios. A fencing club owner cannot advance their students through a recognized sequence or series of belts or grades as students learn and prove their skills through demonstration or club competition. The only way a fencer can earn rankings – which are letter grades – is by participation in national fencing association sanctioned competitions. Because competitions sanctioned by the national fencing association may be – actually are – few and likely far from where a fencer resides, this typically does require a fencer to travel if a fencer desires to be and maintain nationally recognized ranking. Local club competitions are a great way to hone a fencer's skills, but they do not otherwise apply toward a fencer's national ranking grade.

And as long as I am able, I will keep coaching fencing. Inasmuch as I admit that at the time it was a responsibility I did not necessarily want, it is something that I am very glad I accepted. There are certainly benefits beyond fencing that have gone past the expectations, so I suspect that there will be more to come too.

Introduction

Lean Six Sigma is about the continual pursuit of improvement with a goal of the sixth level of sigma: 3.4 defects per million which is to be free of defects 99.99966% of the time. To put this statistic into perspective: according to airline information tracking company SITA (www.sita.aero), in 2018[1] the airlines mishandled just under six pieces (5.69) of luggage per 1,000 passengers. (Airline performance information can also be found at www.transportation.gov for those who are interested.) Extrapolated and rounded up for convenience of discussion, that would be approximately 6,000 mishandles (defects) per one million passengers, which puts this number at about the fourth level of sigma and defect-free only around 99.4% of the time. To think that anything over 99% is pretty darn good would be a generally accurate perspective until the nuances of the numbers really are analyzed and it is your lost luggage that is in the difference.

No entity can simply remain as-is and believe that in doing so it will progress and be a success. A business has to

---

[1]   https://www.sita.aero/resources/type/surveys-reports/baggage-it-insights-2019

take action and advance or it will succumb to the forces that surround it: market changes, competitors, customer demand, economic cycles. (Porter's Five Forces model – Supplier Power, Buyer Power, Competitor Rivalry, Threat of New Entrants, and Threat of Substitution – is a useful framework for an organization to examine its current and future states.) What I have found in my experience is that businesses – and therefore business leaders – too often fail to get to the point of what is causing their chaos and the resultant high operating costs, unhappy customers, quality problems, employee ineffectiveness, inventory issues, software disasters, and useless information, just to name some of the sweeping issues I have encountered at numerous companies I have been employed at or retained by. The distractions take the attention off of the objective. Inefficient motions are a waste of effort and detract from the mark. Brute force exertion – often displayed in business as pride and politics – does not achieve goals, only instead wastes efforts and allows the competitor opponent to gain an edge. Process matters, but so do results: there has to be the right balance and prioritization, and I have witnessed projects go sideways when one is incorrectly forsaken for the other. Inasmuch as this book is a somewhat unique perspective at business problems, it is also a serious strike at what is plaguing businesses small and large, and thus one that I hope each reader will thoughtfully reflect upon during and after reading.

Before We Begin:
Warm-Up Exercise

Greetings! Thank you for stopping by, coming in, and checking things out. As your coach, I will be introducing you to terminologies and definitions you may not be already familiar with as I instruct you on concepts and methodologies in the sport of fencing and their relationship to the intricate world of business. This includes how strategies and tactics used in fencing parallel those that are applied by successful business leaders, managers, and staff who are charged with achieving executional excellence both internally for their fellow employees and externally for their supply chain stakeholders, such as suppliers/vendors (e.g. contract manufacturers, third-party logistics and distribution partners, software companies, and raw material and service providers) and customers.

Normally, if we were at my fencing club, we would be doing some light stretching and warm-up exercises as I would run through some background on the sport of fencing as I am going to be doing momentarily. From a business perspective, you will be learning a lot throughout this book. So, settle in and get comfortable. And if you want to stand

and stretch or move around a little bit while reading, including trying out some of the fencing maneuvers, go right ahead and do so. Just do so safely.

Since this is not actually a book about fencing, some knowledgeable or experienced fencers might find this warm-up chapter a bit of a review. However, for those of you who are not familiar with fencing, I think you will find this overview to be an interesting inside look at a fascinating sport. This background will be beneficial as we proceed with the lessons.

Fencing was one of the original Olympic sports – along with track and field, cycling, swimming, weightlifting, gymnastics, tennis, wrestling, and marksmanship (riflery) – dating back to the first Olympic trials in 1896 and is still a part of Olympic competition today.

Fencing is conducted along a strip (known as a 'piste') which is 14 meters (approximately 38 feet) long and 1.5 to 2 meters (approximately 4 to 5.5 feet) in width. The footwork in fencing is like a weird crabwalk: the fencer is in a crouch position and optimally the fencer moves only from the waist down, keeping the upper part of the body relatively stationary. The footwork is designed to allow the fencer to control speed, distance, and tempo. The fencer's feet do not cross each other in the basic footwork. There is not really a lot of lateral (side-to-side) motion in fencing; the fencer is primarily advancing and retreating forwards and backwards up and down the strip (piste). It is a penalty to go off the piste.

Fencers start by squaring off against each other from the center of the piste out of distance like two boxers in a ring.

Each fencer stands in the '*en garde*' (on guard) ready stance with their weapon held up and facing their opponent. The non-fencing arm cannot be used aggressively during the competition and must stay out of the way the entire time; at no time can the non-fencing arm block the opponent's ability to land their weapon upon target area or interfere with the bout. The non-fencing arm can be used as a counterbalance to movements that the fencer executes, but that is otherwise all.

There are three weapons in competitive fencing: foil, sabre, and epee. Between the three weapons are various similarities and differences, as noted:

- Foil and epee are similar in that they are 'point' weapons because you score a touchpoint with these weapons with the point of the blade. Sabre is a cutting-and-slashing weapon whereby the entire blade can be used to score a touchpoint.

- Foil and sabre are 'right-of-way' weapons. In foil and sabre, the fencer who initiates the attack with an aggressive forward motion, such as the extension of the weapon via the arm or a forward advance, has the right to finish the attack so long as the attack motion is continuous; the opponent, therefore, must defend. Even if the opponent strikes a valid touch against the attacking fencer, if the opponent was on the defensive and the attacking fencer scored a touchpoint immediately afterward within the action motion, the attacking fencer would receive the point.

- Epee has no 'right-of-way' rule, so fencers can attack each other simultaneously and score what is called a 'double-touch' whereby both fencers are considered the attacker and will thus both earn a point if they successfully land their attacks at the same time. An attacking fencer in epee can singularly score and lock-out the other fencer from scoring if their timing is just right too, but the absence of the 'right-of-way' rule increases the risk of the double-touch.

The target areas differ between the three weapons as the following describes:

- The target area in foil is the torso: Essentially, the waist up to the neckline and across to the shoulders (what would be the seams on the outer jacket), front, side, and back.
- The target area in sabre is the foil torso plus the head and the arms down to the wrists (the hands are not included).
- The target area in epee is the entire body, from the top of the head to the tips of the fingers to the tips of the shoes. Absolutely, every aspect of the fencer's body is an open area for target in epee.

A fencer will either attack (in fencing, known as 'attack') or defend (in fencing, known as 'parry'). A 'riposte' is a counter-attack that comes after a fencer has parried (defended) themselves. Parries have numbers assigned to them, e.g. parry four, parry six. Variations on a parry are also numbered, e.g. parry circle-six which is the parry six that includes a circular motion to first capture the opponent's blade before the weapon is moved to the outside of the defending fencer's body position.

The hand holds the weapon, the arm extends the weapon, but much of the maneuvering is done with the wrist, allowing more subtly and less visibly obvious motions to the opponent to be conducted. Circling the weapon around the opponent's blade is a common movement in fencing. An underneath circle is called a disengage. An over-the-top circle is called a coupé. I explain the difference this way: think of a coupé like a government coup, you overthrow a government, e.g. you go over the top. My students find this little memory trick to be an easy way to remember the circle terminology. It's how it was explained to me when I first learned it in fencing.

One of the most basic attack moves there is in fencing is the lunge. It is a power-forward motion where the exertion is from the forceful extension of the back leg. (As I tell my fencing students, the lunge's energy, like the forward footwork motion, comes from the rear-wheel-drive just like the good old American muscle cars of yesteryear, so it requires a push, not pull. Another helpful hint is to have them slightly shift their weight onto their back leg and decrease their crouch stance, similar to a more tightly wound spring or a coiled snake ready to strike.) The lunge extends the attacking fencer and enables the fencer to maximize their reach and previous extension of the weapon arm toward the opponent. From a footwork standpoint, upon landing, the forward leg's knee and toe should be aligned with each other. If the toe is beyond the knee, the fencer has over-lunged. The problem with an over-lunge is that the fencer may now be a sitting duck, unable to recover back to the en garde stance, and this puts the fencer at a competitive disadvantage. Worse, if the fencer has to rock their body forward to push themselves back, this momentarily places their target area closer to their opponent, which is a both a strategic and tactical detriment. If the fencer lunges short where the knee extends beyond the toe of the landed front foot, the fencer's momentum can cause the fencer to fall over themselves, which is just embarrassing.

The fleche maneuver is something like a sudden step-run attack move whereby the attacking fencer ends up past the opponent, the attacking fencer having crossed their legs in stepping passed the opponent in the process while trying to land their weapon upon their opponent's target area. The balestra is like a shuffle-step lunge: a step or two ending sometimes in a small jump is executed prior to the lunge.

The term 'touché' comes from fencing. It is actually exclaimed by the person who is scored upon, who is touched, not by the person who has done the scoring. This is why a person who has had a negative remark spoken against them sometimes replies 'Touché.'

Safety, of course, is the number one priority in my fencing club. Weapon ends (the points) pointed down is the primary rule. And never walk behind a fencer who is engaged in fencing. The speed at which fencing occurs is very fast, and a fencer never looks behind them. You should never turn away from your opponent in fencing, the primary reason is that it exposes the unprotected back of the head to being hit or having a weapon enter the mask from behind, so there is no reason to turn your head to look behind you in fencing. Always maintain a significant distance away from someone who is actively fencing, from behind and from the sides because those weapons have a long reach and, on rare occasions, are known to break and fly off in any direction.

With a bit of background in fencing and now that you are warmed-up, you are ready to begin your lessons.

Lesson One: Are You Equipped to Execute?

As with many sports, the participant's equipment plays a vital role in their capability to perform and execute well. Without the necessary equipment, a person simply would not be able to partake in a particular sport. A cyclist without a bicycle might as well start jogging. But just getting any old equipment is not a sufficient solution. The fit and functionality of the equipment is of primary importance to the participant's being able to use the equipment to their fullest ability and to the equipment's maximum capability.

In fencing, the basic equipment includes the mask, jacket, glove, footwear, chest protector, and weapon. There is additional paraphernalia if a fencer is going to compete, such as body cord, lame (the metallic over-vest or over-jacket in foil and sabre), and wired electric version of the standard 'dry' or practice weapon as well as the electric version of the mask and glove (in sabre) for competition. Fencing knickers (short pants that go down to just below the knee and are held up with suspenders) certainly complete the outfit, but in my club, if someone wears workout pants as we practice that is okay too.

Masks should fit snuggly and comfortably. If the mask is bobbling around on the fencer's head, it is a distraction to the fencer and will negatively affect the fencer's performance. Because the masks are primarily made of a metal mesh, the mask can be gently flexed in or out from side-to-side or top-to-bottom for slight fit adjustment. But overall, the mask itself should be ordered to the correct head size first.

Jacket materials can vary from polyester to heavy cotton canvas, the latter is my personal choice because I believe it protects and breathes better. Jacket styles can be either back zipper – which is a little tricky to maneuver – ladies, I have an appreciation for what you go through, or a front zipper which allows a fencer to conveniently unzip the jacket while not fencing and cool down a bit. The zipper on a front-zip jacket cannot impede the target area acquisition, therefore the zipper on a right-handed jacket is approximately on the outside of the left ribcage area and the zipper on a left-handed jacket is approximately on the outside of the right ribcage area.

Blades, which are made out of steel, can range from rigid to flexible. The advantage of a rigid blade is that it can be more difficult for the opponent to take control of or defend against during an attack due to the greater strength of the blade. The advantage of a flexible blade is that an attacking fencer can actually use a blade's 'whip' as part of maneuvering around an opponent's defending blade in order to score a touchpoint. While forcibly whipping a blade in fencing is poor sport and likely just forbidden to the point of probably resulting in a violation, the fast and strong motions of fencing do cause a natural bend to occur to the steel weapons, especially upon contact. This natural bending – the whip of the blade – can be used offensively by a skilled fencer with a flexible weapon. (My personal preference is a medium-weight steel which affords me the advantage of both strength and flexibility.)

Weapon grips are a real individual preference. There is the French style which is almost straight but with a slight 'S' curve so as to conform to the palm of the hand. Then there are a variety of pistol grip styles that are called such because they more closely resemble the way a gun would be held in the hand or gripped to the palm. Pistol grip styles include Belgium, Hungarian, Visconti, and Russian (my favorite). Different grip styles only apply to foil and epee. There is only one grip style for a sabre.

There are specific shoes made just for fencing, and whether the fencer fences with the right or left hand. On fencing shoes, the shoe opposite the weapon hand has special reinforcing materials because it is on the foot used for lunging, and thus will likely drag on the floor and wear in different places versus the other shoe. I don't use fencing shoes – they are very expensive – so I just purchase flat-on-the-floor athletic shoes on sale. Running shoes are not advisable for fencing because of the cushioning built up on the outside. Fencing is a martial art and all that outside cushioning on running shoes separates the foot from the floor when performing the complicated footwork motions in fencing. Worse, that built-up outer cushioning can be a problem if it causes a person to land incorrectly and turn their ankles resulting in injury.

In business, and as you read this book, consider what equipment is needed to execute the primary function of the company or organization where you work. Granted, a definition of the primary function of the company where you work may have to be reworked before too long, and I hope that this book also helps with that too. But let me start you off easy by saying that the primary function of wherever you work should be to satisfy the customer. Whether it is to provide a service or produce a product, the primary function of so very many companies, most government agencies, and plenty of service organizations, is to satisfy the customer. Some customers are internal to the enterprise, some customers are external to the enterprise. Every process, every software system, should be focused and have as part of its purpose customer satisfaction, whether directly or indirectly. So, how do you need to be equipped – how does your company need to be equipped – to get the job of customer satisfaction done, and done right?

If we take the concept of equipment in the broadest possible sense, it can mean many things: people, processes, machinery, materials, software. People include the executive leaders making what is hoped to be the right decisions and the staff workers who are tasked with carrying out the instructions of the executive leadership, hopefully with the right tools to get the job done. Does the company have documented, clearly defined processes and written procedures for how to do things especially in the event a primary person is not there? Machinery spans the gamut from manufacturing to office equipment. If something is old but critical, are there spare parts at the ready? Is it being maintained on a regular basis, and if not, why? Software systems include Enterprise Resource Planning (ERP), the main business information system of record that virtually all companies rely on to run. Is your company's ERP system up to the task? Is the data representative of the current state? Is your ERP system old and heavily modified? Is your company using all of the ERP system's capabilities, and correctly?

I get it: software projects are expensive and not every company can afford pricey new software. But as I tell the companies I help, you don't always have to: you just need the functionality that you can afford, like the way I purchase shoes for fencing. By clearly defining what is required and what is not and shopping for the available products on the market – sometimes having to look at software products that would not normally be considered but are perfectly suitable for the situation – companies do not have to compromise their requirements to get what they need. Saying this another way: Sometimes you need to look outside your industry for a satisfactory solution. I don't need fencing shoes to be a great fencer, comfortable generic athletic shoes work just fine. This goes for people too: hire a consultant if you can't afford to bring on the employee talent you need.

Lesson Learned

Whether an amateur or competitive athlete or a business, you cannot be successful without the right equipment. But the definition of the 'right' equipment is not completely clear cut: it comes down to price, product capability, and necessary functionality. Selecting the right equipment is the first step to being ready to execute. There is nothing wrong with considering all industry-specific options. However, those should not be the only solutions sought to solve problems if you are going to perform a genuine search. The difficulty is in the realization that external or generic products can be fit or conformed to provide a just-as-good if not even better solution and a better return-on-investment.

Lesson Two: Culture – Style Versus Technique

I don't run my fencing club in an overly rigid manner like a boot camp. That would make it a boring place for me to be as an instructor and my students as participants. I have a gregarious personality and am very spontaneous, both exceptionally useful personal traits in the business world, fencing coaching, and academic instructing. If my fencing club is a chore and I am not having fun, then my students won't have fun either. The result is that my students will not be engaged in the activity and therefore, will not be absorbed in the learning process. Certainly, safety is retained as a priority: just because we are having a good time does not mean we are not having a safe time. (Remember that all new participants are taught the 'points down' rule at the beginning. Also, my participants are taught and reminded not to walk behind or get too close to actively fencing fencers.) There is time for socializing and chatting in between exercises and bouts: I think it is great that my fencing club is a place where the attendees – including the parents – can form social relationships too.

And while we are enjoying ourselves and being safe, the participants are learning how to fence.

No matter the level of skill, all are welcome. I have had parents bring their children who were rejected by coaches at other fencing clubs because their kids were not considered to be competitive-quality, and I think that is terrible. These youngsters found a home at my club and their skills improved under my tutelage. These students' parents told me that their children had a good time and enjoyed being able to participate in a sport that they really did enjoy, which is quite frankly all that mattered. This is part of my club's culture.

Another aspect of my club's culture is the differentiation I make to my students between style and technique. I am sometimes told by my younger students – some who fence with me during the summer while on breaks from their college or university attendance – that their prior or current coaches were or are trying to force them to fence to their coach's style. The student is uncomfortable with this, and in my view, they should be. Even my adults are sometimes surprised to discover that they will have the freedom and flexibility to develop their own fencing style. (Or perhaps I should not be so surprised, as many of them have not participated in a sport like fencing before where they have been one-on-one coached.)

I do not force a student to fence like I do. I do, however, expect a student to execute the movements I show them with the proper technique. There is a big difference between style and technique. I fence in my particular style because it works for me based on my body configuration and my

39

particular strengths and what I am comfortable with. As such, my fencing style is unlikely to work for a whole host of other people. Just because I prefer Russian-style pistol grips on my foils does not mean that my students have to choose that grip style also. In fact, most of my students prefer the French grip after sampling several style types.

When I teach my students a particular move – an attack or parry – I expect them to learn to execute it properly. The move execution technique is exclusive of fencing style: regardless of fencing style, I still expect the move to be executed properly. I allow – and guide – my students in the development of their own fencing style as they figure out what is and is not comfortable for them, and what works and what doesn't necessarily work well for them.

Fencing is well known as a healthful sport as people discuss the athleticism and stamina it must take, and to which I reply that it certainly is a full-body and mentally challenging sport. Fencing is recognized as a graceful sport too, in its movements, speed, and balance requirements. Fencing is associated with chivalry, and why not? Heck, any sport where you can wield a sword is naturally going to be associated with gallantry and courtliness. Whenever I am thanked for holding the door open for a woman, my reply is that chivalry is not dead, it is regrettably in hibernation or taking a long nap. And let's just face the facts: Fencing has its complete 'coolness' factor. There are just not that many fencers around, and any sport that uses a sword is, well, just plain darn cool. Think Star Wars, Pirates of the Caribbean, and Princess Bride for great sword-fighting scenes, (yes, the lightsabers in Star Wars are close enough), let alone the classic Errol Flynn movies of years (sigh, decades) ago. Whenever I tell someone that I teach fencing, it always raises an eyebrow and engages conversation. I don't just participate, I coach, and that ups the discussion bar, not that just being a fencer would not be enough. Fencing is not an elitist sport, it is an exceptional community of people who all share the love of fencing's culture: its disciplines, fun, healthfulness, historical significance, theatrical references, and uniqueness. Fencing is part of me, part of my own unique personal culture.

In business, the culture of an organization needs to be guided by its leaders but must allow the employees the ability to nurture their own talents and creativities. In the Sarbanes-Oxley compliance framework COSO (Committee of Sponsoring Organizations, www.coso.org), which is widely used by public companies and is a great model for private organizations to follow, the setting of the company's culture is the first, and albeit most important, of the five primary aspects. Called the Control Environment, it is also known by its nickname as the 'Tone at the Top.' While not included in the COSO framework, the trickling down of the company's morals, ethics, and values from the senior executives to the middle management is sometimes called the 'Mood in the Middle.'

Is the company culture true and believed or false and patronized? People learn by the example set by the leaders they are supposed to follow and be guided by. If leadership sets a bad example, this bad behavior will be mimicked by employees who will spread the bad conduct internally and externally to outside stakeholders like customers and suppliers/vendors, who may retaliate with their own compromised comportment against the organization out of survival necessity even if it is against their good corporate nature. If employees do not believe in the company, its leaders, its culture, the employees will not execute their individual jobs to the fullest extent possible. Never mind the saying that a chain is only as strong as its weakest link, when the entire chain is weakened the wholesale failure to execute is certainly guaranteed. And when the weak links are the organization's own leaders, the organization itself can only be doomed to failure.

Good company culture should encourage employees to voice their views, cultivate their creativity, and apply their talents to meet the challenges the organization faces head-on. In return, the company cannot just solicit feedback without acknowledgment or putting good ideas into practice without recognizing the source, exploiting the capabilities of its staff. Nor can the company let pride and politics get in the way of letting good ideas and smarter voices be heard, no matter where they come from.

'We talk about making culture a competitive advantage at American,' stated Ralph Lopez, Vice President, American Airlines, in an editorial article printed in the July 19, 2018, Miami Herald newspaper. Company culture is negatively influenced by: ineffective or otherwise disengaged leaders; bad behavior by senior executives; disenfranchised employees; high turnover in the workforce; operational chaos; dysfunctional software systems and infrastructure technology. A good corporate culture will extend outwards and become part of the organization's brand. Customers and suppliers/vendors do tend to pick up on employee emotion in communications (verbal and written) which is impacted by culture. How an organization executes its reason for existence is conveyed to its customers and suppliers/vendors. In the digital age of social media, a company's internal and external performance reputation is able to be transmitted and permeated across the world near instantaneously. Culture matters, whether in the attraction or retention of employees or customers.

I educate companies, from the distribution center to the office to the conference room. I communicate, verbally and in writing, to pass along useful and critical information. I develop siloed departments and fractured areas into cohesive teams that are able to conquer the problems that have previously foiled them. Regrettably, not all companies create a culture of communication that enables this to happen. It is a failure that starts at the top of the organization, and unfortunately one that often prevents success from taking hold and growing.

Lesson Learned

In my fencing club, my instruction is not wholly 'my way or the highway.' I don't impose my style upon my students; rather, I encourage my students to explore their own style based on my instruction in the proper techniques of footwork and weapon work. With the right coaching, in little time even a novice fencer learns to develop their own unique style while still maintaining proper technique and staying within the rules of the club. My students are challenged in fencing with more experienced opponents, but not overwhelmed as the expectation is tempered because they are so new. With their questions, my students challenge me and this makes me a more effective coach. As they develop into being and becoming their own fencers, even with all my instruction, my students find ways to surprise me as we fence together and test each other.

As a leader, I am only delighted by my fencing students' rapid improvement and enjoyment while they participate. As a fellow fencer, I feel great that I have been able to help develop another person who is a member of the fencing community and is able to successfully engage in an activity they enjoy. As a coach, I couldn't be happier in the results of my instruction within the culture I have created that persists within all fencers who join my club. I have the confidence that I am developing effective fencers who are ready to take on the challenges that they will face on the fencing strip.

So, within my fencing club, there is certainly a hierarchy as I am the owner and the coach. I have simple safety rules which must be followed at all times. I allow my fencers to develop their own style, but expect them to execute the moves with the right technique. This describes the culture of my fencing club. Put professionally, I mentor but I don't mold.

In a business, there will similarly be an organizational hierarchy, but how will this hierarchy impose its will upon the rest of the company? How will the leaders at the top develop and communicate their desires to the middle management who will then rally the staff-level troops to get the work done? Is the company culture suffering from the pains of operational inefficiencies or software system struggles? Does leadership have plugged ears and blinders on to the real problems or concerns of the working staffers?

In my professional experience, I strive to elevate the leaders and employees at companies to become more functional individuals and therefore create a more effective organization that is better capable of executing its primary purpose. I try to open their eyes to the real problems, the root causes of chaos, and solution suggestions. Organizations, in creating their culture, should differentiate between style and technique in the development of its employees. To squash creativity and innovation and uniqueness, to silence voices, is to restrain the organization from realizing its true potential and to restrict it from meeting and beating the competitive market forces. As this book discusses later, your organization has got resources, you just need to realize them and utilize them.

Lesson Three:
Engagement for Interest

As a coach, I show my students the basics and advanced techniques of fencing, including my little tips and tricks that I use myself. But I do not try and mold my students to my style. Instead, I let my students develop their own style, ask questions, and try new moves, even allowing them to make up a new move of their own design. (I can only imagine what traditional fencing instructors and masters are thinking of that last statement. I see no harm in allowing students to explore their creativity, and then we discuss the pros and cons of why such a move would or would not be practical. It is all part of the learning experience in my opinion.) I foster my students to evolve into becoming their own fencers. As long as they execute the moves I instruct them with the right technique, which is essentially style-independent, their style is their own.

To keep my students interested, we don't just go through boring drills over and over and over again. Ugh. That would be repetitive and dull-as-dishwater for both the instructor (me) and the student (them). Certainly, practice drills have their place: namely, at the beginning when learning something new, or doing some warm-up exercises. But to constantly be doing drill after drill after drill is just too tedious. I would rather do something fun where I can learn as I go along, and my students feel the same way. By keeping it interesting I keep my students engaged, and the learning comes somewhat naturally.

My style of instructing is to show the student the maneuver, dissecting it into its constituent parts. We go slowly and methodically so the student can follow every minor move I make and copy what I do to replicate the technique. I need the student to understand why each step in the maneuver is important, so we examine the analytical aspects of the moves, including pros and cons of altering a move or why one option works better than another. Sometimes, I will go into detail as to whether one movement selection may be preferable depending on whether the opponent is right-handed or left-handed. Remember: because I am ambidextrous, I naturally have more than one perspective in fencing.

(In my professional work, I am able to bring together multiple viewpoints when problem solving because of my abilities to analyze data, investigate business operations, measure supply chain performance, and examine software systems.)

We practice, slowly at first so the student can acclimate to the maneuver's moves and counter-moves, getting used to the how their muscles feel in the rest of their body, checking their stance and footwork. We'll then speed up as the student becomes more comfortable with the maneuver. I'll add in some complexity, e.g. we shift from executing the maneuver from a standing position to doing so with footwork motion up and down the fencing strip. I will then encourage the student to add the maneuver into their repertoire and use it during their regular course of fencing. Practice, after all, makes perfect.

The methodology here is to introduce the student to the maneuver, have the student understand the maneuver in its detailed steps, work through some trial and error, and incorporate the maneuver into the student's standard routine as soon as possible. Naturally, the student will still require instruction and continued practice to master the maneuver, but better that the student should get this experience in actual fencing bouts rather than just through continual drills is my opinion and experience. Theory is great, but application really proves the concept.

As a university adjunct instructor, I was tasked with teaching a technology basics class that included Microsoft Word and Microsoft PowerPoint. Quite frankly, there is nothing very captivating about learning these software products for university students. The book series and accompanying study software I was provided to use had rather straightforward lessons and uninspiring exercises. The students were not very engaged in the coursework's mandatory lessons. Fortunately, I had wide discretion as to how I taught the class and used the teaching software.

I decided to use the teaching software assignments as the in-class lecture and assigned the students a cleverly devised build-a-business project I conceived of that would be a significant portion of their grade. They would pick any legitimate business idea they wanted and create a business, including: a name, color scheme, font, mission statement, and marketing tag line. In Microsoft Word, they would create their own business card and marketing brochure based on the lessons I would teach them. In Microsoft PowerPoint, they would create a prototype web site for their business, again, based on some of the lessons I would teach them. (The students also had another presentation project using PowerPoint as a standard presentation tool.) I incorporated real-world experiences from my own business career into the build-a-business project. Because the students knew of my professional background which I reviewed with them on the first day of the school term, they appreciated the fact that I was bringing real-world knowledge into the classroom.

For the vast majority of students, the creative project to build a business of their choosing was something that they really enjoyed and gravitated to. The project really brought out a lot of creativity and skill from many of the students. Some students just had a fun time and let their imaginations go wild. Other students did a good deal of research and brought forth some quite intriguing – and I think inspiring – potential business ideas. Some students created projects based on deep passions they had from personal situations they encountered or endured while growing up, and I think that sharing these experiences with their classmates really took a lot of fortitude. I encouraged several students to enter their ideas in the university's business concept challenge.

Because my university students were engaged, they were interested. Their projects were overall very successful and for many of them earned top grades. Inasmuch as a lot of them didn't like publicly presenting their projects to the class, it was a good experience and I did not downgrade them for any lack of public speaking skills. My students were strictly graded on whether they used the techniques I instructed them on to accomplish their tasks, and if they went farther in adding their own style and creativity to what they did.

At one company I helped, an over-bearing supervisor did a great job of diminishing the opinions of a younger, newer, and therefore inexperienced employee who eventually was so brow-beaten by the supervisor that she became reluctant to speak up and say what was on her mind. That changed when I began my consulting assignment and started to engage her like a professional, and she intelligently discussed with me her perceptions about what was going on. Granted, she was young and inexperienced at the time, but she proved to me to be an invaluable asset and assisted me greatly with her insights into what she did know, which was more than she thought.

(An important lesson is to never discount someone just because of their age or otherwise outward appearance. A portly fencer may not be able to move as quickly but may have superior weapon technique and can handily defeat someone with lesser-developed skills who yet may be swifter on their feet.)

On one occasion, this particular young and not-as-experienced person, as the months went by, informed me of a situation with how damaged inventory was – or actually, was not – being recorded in the company's business software when the company's third-party logistics warehouses sent in email notifications, as that is where the trail ended. In essence, the company's multiple contract warehouses were informing the company via the only way they knew and were instructed how – by email – of inventory damages but no adjustments were being made within the company's Enterprise Resource Planning (ERP) system, the business operations and accounting software system of record. It was no wonder why the inventory on-hand quantity and value in the company's ERP software was offset and higher versus at all the contract warehouses: the damages had never been deducted, having been left to sit in an email folder.

The company was well-aware of this supervisor's belligerent attitude toward other employees, but did not do anything to mitigate, or as is sometimes necessary, eliminate the attitude problem. But just as bad, the actual knowledgeable employee was never engaged for interest, and so she kept her mouth shut until she was properly approached like a professional. The result was that for nearly one full year the company's inventory was inaccurate, negatively affecting its abilities to successfully fulfill orders, plan manufacturing, and keep its customers happy.

Like so many situations I have encountered with the companies I have helped, this problem was not resolved until an outside person – me – was brought in to perform discovery and professionally interact with those who actually knew what was going on but were never engaged and, in this instance, were actually disengaged and disenfranchised from speaking up when they knew something was wrong and damaging to the enterprise.

For business organizations, it is not enough to simply include in the company culture continuing education reimbursements, unless the company is looking to improve its employees until they walk right out the door. Nor does the company culture stop at clever quips posted on the walls. Mission statements and value propositions are useless and worse, become unfulfilled promises (translation: lies), if company leaders do not uphold the meaning behind what they have committed to in writing. Organizations must engage their employees as part of their culture, embracing continual education and training but then allowing the employee to be effective and heard upon completion of that learning experience.

Executives should be meeting regularly with office and distribution center staff. But executives cannot just let these be lip-service sessions: employees need to be allowed to say what is on their mind without fear of repercussion or criticism, and executives should listen carefully and truly consider each employee's thoughts, perceptions, and suggestions before discounting them. When an employee's idea is implemented, the employee should be recognized and appropriately rewarded or compensated, e.g. if the idea saved the company money or increased sales.

Organizations can foster employees to be more respectfully forthright and 'say something when they see something' if the company creates a culture that nurtures this type of encompassing behavior. Inasmuch as a job is a place to work, that does not mean that an employee does not have to feel that they are not invested in their company too. But for this ownership to happen, the employee must be interested enough to want to be engaged and be part of the organization.

In its annual survey of employee engagement, the Gallup (www.gallup.com) organization's statistics are a rather consistent reminder of how organizations are constantly taking one step backward for every two steps forward, and how most employees are not pulling their own weight, perhaps because they are not engaged or encouraged to do so, or see no reason why they should bother to try. In 2016, Gallup found that 33% of employees were engaged in their jobs, 49% of employees were not engaged in their jobs, and 18% of employees were disengaged from their jobs. These statistics vary little from the 2015 numbers which found that 32% of employees were engaged, 51% were not engaged, and 17% were disengaged. Even going back to 2006, Gallup's numbers do not vary much from the current indicators: 29% of employees were engaged, 56% were not engaged, and 15% were disengaged. Engaged employees are the ones driving innovation and leading the organization forward; not engaged employees are the warm bodies who are doing work but are not really progressing the company forward, though they are not holding the company back; however, the disengaged employee's actions are thwarting the positive efforts of the organization and are causing chaos and disruption.

I don't tolerate disruptive behavior in my fencing club, because that typically translates into unsafe situations, aside from creating an environment where the main purpose of the fencing club – learning to fence – is compromised. The acceptance of disruptive behavior in the workplace typically translates into a stressful workplace environment for other employees and has an additional adverse effect of increasing operating costs due to inefficient or ineffective procedures and compromised data governance which results in inaccurate information leading to incorrect decisions being made.

Lesson Learned

In business, when mentoring less experienced employees, or coaching executives, it is important to give them assignments and opportunities to use what they have learned plus what they have buried within them that is waiting for the chance to come out and be used. The purpose should not be to have the other person replicate you – the instructor – but rather to have you guide them to be better at what they do. This is done by placing a weapon – literal or figurative – in their hands and guiding them on how to wield it. The weapon may be a sword or it may be a methodology. How you teach is just as important as what you teach in getting the lesson across and having it be accepted.

I never told my university students what colors or fonts or templates to use: I provided guidance and suggestions and let them run wild with their imaginations. The results were often an absolute impressive joy and every bit as professional as work I have seen produced by paid experts. I never wanted my students to match my style, only to follow proper constructive technique in using the software, albeit differently than how they imagined it could be used, which was a revelation to them itself.

Ensure you create an environment where everyone can learn and equally participate. If you make sure that everyone is actively engaged, the benefits of that engagement will flow in multiple directions: the participant (e.g. student, employee) will benefit, the organization (e.g. club, company) will benefit, the associates (e.g. in a club, the other students and their parents; in a company, the customers, and suppliers/vendors) will benefit. Execution – personal or professional, individual or organizational – will improve under the right engagement.

Lesson Four: Do the Foundational Stuff First

When I acquire a new fencing student, I first do a general review of fencing for about 20 minutes. It is an overall conversation about fencing as a sport. I offer a wide-ranging overview of the sport of fencing, essentially covering what I provided to all of you in my warm-up chapter in this book. I think it is important to provide a comprehensive understanding to the student of what the sport is about and what they are getting themselves involved with.

The first aspect of fencing I teach my new students is footwork, not weapon handling. Granted, the footwork part is not as exciting as the weapon work. It is, however, foundationally fundamental that the new students establish their proper footwork early on for several very good reasons. With footwork comes along the also important body posture.

First, the footwork is awkward. The martial-arts style of footwork in fencing is not necessarily easy to gravitate to. (I describe the footwork in more detail later in the book.) Trust me when I tell you that great weapon handling won't help much without proper footwork skills which includes correct body stance, center of balance, and good foot positioning. Because a fencer can defend with weapon and with distance, the need to be able to move one's feet fast is a necessity in being able to both attack the opponent when within striking distance and protect oneself by backing out of the way. If a fencer cannot maintain their footwork, balance, and body posture they risk fumbling around, tripping over their own feet, failing to move out of the way, the inability to maintain target focus, or forfeiting the capability to use speed, distance, and tempo as part of their resources.

Second, the footwork needs to become autonomic, like breathing. Weapon work, on the other hand, is conscious thought even though defensive maneuvers can become intuitive reactions for experienced fencers. When someone is coming at you with a metal sword, you are not actively thinking about the positions of your feet or the width of your stance: you just expect those nuances of your footwork to be engaged, correct, and working. This being said, I admit that I am as aware of my footwork as I need to be, but what I am stating here is accurate: my footwork is essentially automatic and self-correcting, and this is good because there is a whole lot of action going on above the waist that involves swords of steel that I need to worry about.

Third, footwork is easy to practice at home. When I first learned how to fence, I would practice my footwork for about 20 minutes each day most days of the week. This involved my forward advances and backward retreats, as well as my lunges. I encourage my students to perform these simple practice exercises at home. They are also a great way to build up the leg muscles needed for fencing. And for those new students who are struggling with their stamina, these exercises at home will help improve their overall athletic performance. So, the sooner I introduce footwork and get the students to start practicing footwork at home, the sooner the student can become more accomplished at this aspect of fencing.

Fourth, admittedly footwork just is not as cool or interesting as weapon work. As such, if a student is willing to stick it out for a lesson or two with just the footwork, then it is a good indication that they are more than just a little serious about learning fencing. With their interested tested, I have a better idea if they will return or not, and what kind of student they will be if or when they next do show up. Starting with footwork is somewhat of a new participant litmus test too, but this is the least important of all of the reasons to begin with footwork over weapon handling.

In business, getting the foundational stuff out of the way first creates a clearer path toward the goals and allows for a better chance of cleaner execution of plans and projects. Sometimes it is just part of common-sense project management, such as performing a clean-up of data prior to the implementation of a new software system. I cannot imagine why anyone would not want to update their existing data to be more conducive for the current state of the organization and to support the pending future state before uploading it to a brand-new software system, yet some organizations fail to adequately perform this task. This is analogous to purchasing a brand-new automobile and running it on old, outdated gasoline or oil. That just does not make any sense.

Organizations tend to do a very poor job of identifying – let alone documenting – their operating procedures. As such, what they fail to discover is that people are wasting a lot of time and effort – translation: money – in performing repetitive or redundant (wasteful) tasks because an initial baseline task was either not performed or performed out-of-sequence. Not only are people's time consumed unnecessarily, but resources such as paper and toner or email or disk drive space (which seems to be unlimited but really is not) may be needlessly expended in the process.

Lesson Learned

It is not enough to just identify the steps within a maneuver or business process, the sequential order of those steps has to be such that the entirety of the whole is built upon a solid foundation. Each successive step is built upon the previous step. If there is no direct relationship, question the purpose of performing a step. In fencing, building weapon lessons upon the establishment of good footwork ensures that the student will start off with the proper body stance and balance to handle their sword when the time comes. Good footwork skills are a necessity to enable the fencer to advance and retreat, changing direction as a reflection of the needs of the bout and in reaction to the opponent's actions.

Businesses are constructed of complex and interrelated activities that are comprised of simpler jobs. Getting the building block tasks correct and in the right order creates a foundation upon which the organization is able to grow. If a change in direction is necessary, the company should be able to easily accomplish this because it will be on solid footing first and foremost. This groundwork, therefore, creates the ability to be more agile, whether in business or in fencing. Before a company tries to handle the complicated, it needs to be able to master the easy in order to successfully execute.

Lesson Five:
Build upon the Basics

As a fencing coach, I establish a foundation of skills in footwork and basic weapon work before moving on to more advanced maneuvers. I want my students to be successful in their journey to becoming a fencer. To teach too much too quickly will overwhelm a student, especially a new student at that. The instruction has to be paced on an individual basis. I have an educational plan that I know works well in developing new students and enhancing even experienced fencers.

With footwork, learning how to move up and down the fencing strip – to move forward and reverse, advance and retreat – before I teach a student how to lunge helps to establish proper foot positioning, balance, and body stance first. In weapon work, I teach new students how to defend themselves before I teach them how to attack. Within the defensive and offensive maneuvers, I stick to a few basic moves for several weeks before I introduce more complex options. Distance is an advanced technique in fencing that can be a powerful strategy both defensively and offensively when one knows how to use it. Students, especially children, need extra training time to get their heads wrapped around how to incorporate distance into everything they are learning. The concept of distance is more intuitive for adults than it is for children.

When students ask about which weapon they should learn first, I always tell them they should start with foil. The first reason is that of the three weapons, I don't teach epee, so let's strike that one. The second reason is that foil is probably the best technique weapon of all three: it has the smallest target area and, like epee, is a point weapon (meaning that you have to score with the point, not like sabre where you can score with any part of the blade), so precise accuracy to target is without compromise. The third reason is that foil hurts the least of the three weapons: sabre is a cutting-and-slashing weapon and epees are rather stiff and the jabs can be felt more forcefully than foil. Quite frankly, some students – especially children – just don't like getting hit, even while wearing protective gear. (Author's note: I have never lost a student to injury or worse.) Fourth, it is possible to use some of what is learned in foil (and probably epee) in sabre, but I don't find that the weapon work in sabre translates back as naturally into a point weapon like foil. So, if you start in foil and then want to learn sabre, there are some basic weapon skills in foil that will transfer over nicely to sabre.

In business, without the foundational basics, perfect execution will not be achievable. A software system will never produce the necessary results if the baseline data (e.g. customers, items, vendors; bills of material, labor, and operations) was never established that favorably supports the business. Similarly, data governance for the entry of business entities (e.g. customers, items, vendors) and transactions (e.g. sales orders, purchase orders, work orders, invoices) must be established such that the transactions adhere to the company's business rules and the software system's business logic. Operational procedures have to start with the initial steps and progress in a logical order. While this last statement may seem to be so implicit that it could not be anything but true, you would be surprised at how inefficient I find companies to be due to haphazard and convoluted business processes. There is a difference between sequenced steps and organized steps that build upon themselves in a complementary way, such as an efficient product assembly process. Just because there is a list does not imply what is listed is done so in a logical or organized manner.

With the basics established to be built upon, the successes of those basics should be easily repeatable. The motion becomes less of a forethought and more of an afterthought as the movement becomes intuitive. Confidence level is improved with each repeated success. More confidence brings increased engagement. The more the successes are repeated, the more the failures are eliminated due to improved confidence, better skill, and greater overall understanding.

Once the basics are well established, experimenting with more complex options or variations is easier. The student will be less apprehensive to try new maneuvers due to their inability to grasp the foundational concepts or confusion with being taught too much too quickly. Each fencer will eventually assemble their own style and gravitate toward moves they are most comfortable with. Some fencers may delay adding a particular move to their repertoire until later because of an initial discomfort with the maneuver. Some fencers may never bring a particular maneuver into their style of fencing. I do not fleche as it just does not seem to work with my low-crouch stance style of fencing. I prefer my feet to be in contact with the floor as much as possible, giving me the maximum amount of control when I need it, always there ready to rely on it. But it is each fencer's own choice to decide what does and does not work for them as they become knowledgeable and experienced and experiment with what does and does not work well for their fencing style.

In business, the organization should first embrace and excel at what it is good at doing. There may certainly be temptations to branch off and try different pathways of business ventures, e.g. different product or service ideas. However, not every business will be successful in every aspect of the industry within which they serve. Law firms typically specialize in a few branches of the law. Physicians are specialists, even if they are general practitioners. The information technology field is divided into disciplines such as infrastructure (e.g. networks), cyber, business software, and online (e.g. web sites). Begin at the basics: what can the company succeed at doing, and be a success at doing rather quickly? This will bring in needed revenue to cover operating costs, help build a positive brand reputation, and get the company experience in being a business.

To believe that a business can be-all and do-all is really beyond normal expectation. While I am not one to throw cold water on anyone's dreams, even the world's largest online retailer started out as a 'simple' bookseller. Starting from what a company knows how to do well and can be successful at, determine what other maneuvers can be worked into the business model repertoire. And don't think that every single move needs to be fit in to be successful.

Lesson Learned

I fully understand the impatience that new fencers feel when they ask me the question 'How long before I really learn how to fence?' or 'How long before I become a great fencer?' The best answer I can give them is that it depends upon the person and how hard they want to work at it. It also depends upon how well they listen and learn. I tell them that they have to start with the basics – like I did – before they can learn the advanced skills like they see me doing.

Businesses are no different. Organizations that fail to establish a solid foundation of people, procedures, data structures, and software systems are doomed to crumble due to the inability to build upon the basic needs of a modern-day enterprise. Organizations that stray too far from their core competency product or service are likely to meet the same fate of failure unless they establish a basic foundation of capability upon which to build their new business venture.

I am not averse to trying and learning – and not succeeding at – new things. My cautionary tale here is that there is simply no reason to run the high risk of execution failure or suffering learning disappointment by putting results ahead of process, emphasizing the process without consideration of the results, or placing both before the basics. Building upon a foundation ensures that education and experimentation work together at each and every step to create success for the current and successive step. If a step does advance you toward a goal, it was likely a step worth taking. Embrace what works for your company and do not feel the pressure to include what your company is not good at executing, especially not until you have practiced, gotten really good at the basics, and are ready to add it to your professional repertoire.

Lesson Six: Process and Results Both Matter

Which is more important: the process or the result?

Certainly, results are important. In fencing, a scoring touchpoint is successfully completed only when a good hit to target is made. How that hit was executed is not part of the consideration as long as nothing prohibited was done in the process, e.g. you cannot throw your sword at the opponent, nor would you want to ever give up your weapon especially in such a manner. However, this all being said, a sloppy execution leaves a fencer wide open to being susceptible to being scored upon in the process (in fencing what is known as the 'preparation') of their attack. Or, should a fencer's attack fail or suddenly cease, a poor process leaves them less likely to mount a successful parry (defense) and a potential return with a riposte (counter-attack), leaving the attacking fencer vulnerable to a successful strike by their opponent.

When I teach attacks, I teach the process of the attack. I do this because there is an inherent belief in students that an attack has to be completed and as it was intended, and this is wholly untrue. Firstly, an attack can be diverted to another target area if the original target area becomes unattainable due to an opponent's expected or unexpected defensive move, but the attacking fencer sees another open target area that is believed to still be achievable to reach while in the attack motion. (Likely the new target area opened up because the opponent maneuvered their weapon to defend the attack and created a new open pathway to a different target area.) However, secondly, an attack can be halted should a fencer encounter a situation, such as a well-executed defensive maneuver by an opponent, (e.g. one that captured the attacking fencer's weapon, the opponent moved out of distance), which renders the attack unwise or unachievable in the opinion of the attacking fencer.

An attack in fencing begins with forward motion or movement toward the opponent. A fencer has to be within striking distance for the opponent to be threatened and for the attacking fencer to be effective. In foil, I prefer a traditional style of attack in which my weapon-holding arm is fully extended. I want to keep my target area – in foil, it is my torso – as far away from my opponent as possible. A fully extended arm allows me to accomplish this. I also want to avail myself of all possible protective strategies I have at my disposal: a fully extended weapon arm allows me to use distance and shield (the weapon's bell guard which, with a fully extended arm, is now centered between me and my opponent) defensively.

(Author's note: When I attack in sabre, I also extend my weapon arm to my opponent while I am advancing, maintaining this protective distance between my opponent and my target area. In sabre, the target area is the upper body: torso, arms (but not the hands), and the head. As such, the timing of my arm extension in sabre and foil is a little bit different. In sabre, depending upon the attack I am executing, I am sometimes literally pushing my weapon into my opponent, encountering and blocking my opponent's weapon, and then closing my attack with a wrist action, all in a single, nonstop, constant motion. In my style of fencing, distance is something I use to my advantage. I will discuss distance and the related topic of perspective later in the book.)

In moving forward first or making the first aggressive motion, I establish the right to attack, known in foil and sabre as the right-of-way. I have the right to continue the attack as long as my aggressive motions are continuous and I do not withdraw the attack, e.g. back away from my opponent or withdraw my weapon from the extension. However, I am not bound by any rule to proceed with the attack. If, in an analysis of the situation – in calibrating my opponent – I do not believe that continuing the execution of the attack is beneficial, I should simply cease the continuation of the attack. This is part of the attack process decision tree.

As I attack, if I were to continue the attack, and depending upon the attack I am executing, I may have to circle my weapon, in a disengage (underneath circle) or coupé (over-the-top circle) pattern, around my opponent's defending weapon. But before I do that, I have a choice: I could opt to end my attack or continue it. This is also part of the attack process decision tree.

I may have wanted to attack a particular target spot on my opponent but due to how the opponent opted to defend, I needed to make a quick alteration to my attack vector. Upon circling around my opponent's weapon, if the new trajectory was not a clearly convincing path that I felt I could be successful with, there is no requirement that I continue my attack (most likely with a closing lunge); I could withdraw it at that moment. This is, again, part of the attack process decision tree.

(Author's note: At each juncture described above where I would have halted my attacks, my next move would have most likely been to increase my distance to the opponent and return to the en garde stance, ready to relaunch an attack or defend an incoming strike by the opponent. Another option would be to hold my ground and force the opponent to retreat which would have still been a territorial win for me. Fencers do play the real estate game on the strip in trying to force their opponents into their respective piste ends to increase pressure, minimize maneuverability, and possibly force the opponent off the end of the strip which is a violation.)

Factors that are involved in the attack/no-attack decision process include: distance, speed (mine, my opponent's), weapon position (mine, my opponent's), my opponent's open target area, my judgment of my opponent's capabilities. Because fencing is such a fast sport, all of this is happening within seconds, perhaps a fraction of a second sometimes if it is the determination of a go/no-go decision.

The above foil or sabre (or epee – target area the entire body, head to toe – I don't want to leave fencers of that weapon out of the conversation) attack process could be documented in a flow chart. The process is critically important to understand because it is not necessary to always complete an attack; in fact, it can be detrimental to have the mindset that an attack has to always be completed. I want my students to understand how to react to change and to be successful in reacting to change.

Businesses too often forget that it is okay to admit that a go-forward plan did not pan out or execute well and should be terminated. Effectively, that the business was attacking an idea and the attack failed or should have been halted but was left to continue unwisely. New products, new services, new software systems: I have witnessed companies lose tens of thousands, hundreds of thousands, and multi-millions of dollars due to poor execution and damn-the-torpedoes commitment because they refused to admit that their attacks – their ideas or plans – were ill-conceived and they plowed ahead to the sometimes utter and unnecessary destruction of the company itself.

I once halted a multi-year, multi-million-dollar custom software project. Over the course of two years, a company had spent approximately – actually, it was just over – four million dollars with an outsourced software team to develop what was initially a warehouse management system but then morphed into a full-fledged sales order processing, accounting, inventory, invoicing, and call center system. After attempting to go live twelve times, (yes, twelve as in 'one dozen'), the software system literally could not correctly add the details on a packing list and have it sum to the calculated total. Mathematics is something that computers do quite well and have done so for many decades. After the final straw which was go-live attempt number twelve, I was brought in to the project, (I was already consulting there on a supply chain matter), and encouraged the owners and senior executives to cancel this fiasco, which they agreed they should have done a long time ago. It took me two weeks of investigations and meetings but at the end of that period of time the failed software project was canceled and the inept software team was fired. I was asked to help lead the company through a new ERP software selection and implementation project which we accomplished successfully in the following twelve months, avoiding any significant customizations or modifications to the selected software. The new project price was one-quarter of the total expended – and wasted – on the runaway custom software project.

New products, services, markets, and channels are always targets that businesses should be willing to explore. New software systems, updated machinery, and new business processes are investments that businesses must be willing to undertake to support new opportunity targets. But the results won't work out unless the path to target is thought through, including possible exit points if there is a legitimate need or practical decision that requires halting a plan for the protective good of the organizational body. And the sooner one can exit an attack, the less scathed and scarred one is to return to battle the next time around.

Lesson Learned

Repeatable processes always work well until change happens, and if you don't know how to critically think and respond to change and the unexpected, which is a natural part of the real world, you will not be prepared for the reality of business. Businesses cannot simply document processes and forget about what happens when changes occur. Process documentation needs to be updated, but also contingency plans need to be considered for when things don't always go according to plan. It is okay to cancel an attack at the early stages if there is obvious evidence that continuing forward is going to be ineffective or lead to disastrous results. It is when attacks – or business plans – are left to continue due to pride, politics, or other forms of failed leadership that organizations suffer needlessly and are unable to successfully defend against the repercussions. Of course, proper planning aids in successful execution and avoidance of attack failures. This is part of what else is discussed in this book, so keep reading.

It is also important to note that there cannot be so much focus on the process that the purpose is lost. The process is critically important, ask anyone who focuses on compliance frameworks like Sarbanes-Oxley where how you get to the results matters as much (if not more) as the results themselves. But when the process eclipses the results purely for the selfish sake of the process versus the product, it becomes time to re-evaluate the process's place in the priority of things.

At some point, a fencer needs to attack: that is the result of the process. During my studies for my Lean Six Sigma

Black Belt, the course authors were transparent in mentioning that one of the known criticisms of lean projects in their pursuit of continuous improvement is that they are in continuous pursuit: it is a never-ending process which, at some point, many businesses have little money and patience for. There comes a time when there is a diminishing return whereby more money invested in the process does not balance the results gained. A fencer cannot continue to prepare for an attack without becoming subject to being attacked and scored upon: the fencer will just wear themselves out physically and it leaves them vulnerable: their weapon becomes out of position to be useful defensively, their mindset is focused solely on attack and never on defend, and they are likely in close enough proximity to their opponent to be a target threat.

Software project management is another area of concern where processes may not be delivering the needed results. If the project management methodology is aligned toward showcasing completed projects without delivering the needed internal or external customer results, then the project methodology has essentially been an exercise in futility, satisfying the project participants while leaving the product owners in a state of frustration. Just as in fencing, speed and agility are all well and good, and whether you proceed forward in a sprint or lunge can become a matter of semantics, but delivery of the right results is what ultimately matters. Remember: in business, it is all about the customer, and customers exist internally and externally to the enterprise. The end result is that the target needs to be hit to score a point.

A process for the sake of a process does no good. A process with an end purpose achieves results. The process can and should include an exit strategy at key junctures because plan as we might, unintended and uncontrolled things will happen. This gives us the chance to recover, reset, and return.

Results matter, as do how we get to the results. There has to be a balance between the two – results and process – to ensure that at no time are we stuck on a wrong path without an exit or that we forget why we are on the pathway at all.

Lesson Seven: Variety Is the Spice of Sport

Did you know that some ice hockey, basketball, and soccer players will take ballet lessons to improve strength and balance? (Ballet reportedly – based on various opinions – originated in Italy in the 15th and 16th centuries, apparently, as the dance interpretation of fencing. Wow – interesting!) It is generally regarded as a good idea to participate in multiple, complementary sports rather than to stick with only one sport. Complementary sports help to build muscles a single sport may not build and to provide an overall better conditioning routine. Participation in the same sport too much without building complementary muscles can have a detrimental effect in the wear-and-tear of those overused muscles, and well as a potential knock-on effect on the surrounding joints, ligaments, and tendons.

I don't just participate in fencing: I used to be a soccer player; an avid bicyclist enjoying 20-mile rides at a clip; a jogger; a racquetball player. Now I focus on my fencing and enjoy my strength training and cardio exercises.

In the July 29, 2018, Miami Herald newspaper article on children's health, Nicklaus Children's Hospital pediatric orthopedic surgeon Dr. Craig Spurdle states that cross-training is important because different muscles are used to enable the body to handle the effect of the athlete's primary sport. In other words – and I don't need to be a doctor to understand this – focusing only on the same activity is actually detrimental to excelling at that activity. And if it's good guidance for children to build a foundation on, I have no doubt, it's wise advice for adults too.

In business, it is well known that it takes multiple talent sets and people with different perspectives for an organization to be successful. Ensuring that there is a gender balance in meetings helps to guarantee that one-sided perspectives do not overshadow decisions. As a business professional with multiple disciplines (data analyst, software expert, operations specialist, supply chain authority) and credentials (Lean Six Sigma Black Belt, Certified Fraud Examiner, Certified Controls Specialist, Microsoft Office Specialist), with experience in different industries, I provide the companies I help with a comprehensive and complementary set of skills based on a solid foundation of experience that they would normally have to hire several people to replicate. The benefit is a multi-faceted perspective in solving business problems, one in particular that came directly out of one of my fencing clubs.

One of my fencers – an adult – was coming to class very frustrated for several weeks and it was negatively affecting her performance. I don't always like to get involved in my club participants' personal or professional lives too deeply, though it is natural that conversations will stray into the

'What do you do for a living?' area at some point, or we will discuss what we did over the weekend, holiday plans, or vacation trips with significant others will enter into the discussion. I like my fencing club's social aspect as part of its culture. For the purpose of my retelling of the tale, I'll refer to my fencer as Judy, which is definitely not her real name.

Initially, Judy just did not want to discuss what was bothering her, so I certainly did not push the issue as it was obviously a sensitive topic. Eventually, though, she revealed to me that her employer had been audited and severely penalized for their lack of fixed asset management across multiple office locations. Not only was this bad, but this was not the first time her organization had failed the audit for fixed asset management, thus the severe penalty they were assessed.

I queried Judy a little bit about her business situation. After learning more about the problem, I informed her about what I did for a living and that I was confident I had a solution for their woes. In disbelief, Judy rather shook this off. I offered to stop by her office any time and chat with her and whomever she wanted in a meeting to explain my proposed solution, but there was no acknowledgment to my offer from Judy.

For the next several successive weeks – Judy's attendance was consistent – Judy was obviously growing more despondent about the situation at her workplace. It was apparent that her accountability for this fixed asset project was putting a lot of strain on her. I knew that Judy was a senior executive in the organization's information technology department, so she had a lot of responsibility. Finally, after fencing one night soon thereafter, Judy literally cornered me and asked me how I would solve the problem. I informed her that I had solved a very similar inventory problem for luxury hotel just a short number of months earlier, and that the principles and technology (software and hardware) of inventory control and fixed asset management were very comparable. Intrigued, fatigued, and exasperated, Judy asked me if I would come by her office for a meeting, to which of course I happily agreed.

In my subsequent meeting with Judy, the purchasing director, and the accounting controller, I explained how I would solve the problem with a simple software solution that mimicked what I did for inventory control at the luxury hotel. The group was collectively stunned: not only was my solution one-tenth of the price of a system being forced upon them by an outside firm with industry political influence, but my solution was easier to implement, easier to integrate to the main software system, and provided some enhanced interim audit reporting that the forced solution could not. It was a literal no-brainer and we proceeded to move forward with a contract. The project was a big success.

As revealed by the group in the first meeting, they simply didn't see the solution from any other perspective. The similarity between inventory and fixed assets never crossed their minds, even though Judy's organization has a warehouse with an inventory control system which I later upgraded as a separate project. The politically motivated solution was being pushed regardless of whether it was the right solution or not, let alone whether it was good or not. (Apparently, according to Judy, based on their evaluation, it was neither.) It was not until variety was added – me – that the best solution to the problem came to the forefront.

Lesson Learned

Just as the repetition of doing the same thing over and over again becomes boring and tiresome and can be wearing on muscles which can result in aches and pains, adding variety brings much-welcomed spice, retains interest, and builds complementary muscles that improve overall performance both physically and mentally. Businesses need to understand that not all of their problems can be solved by solely relying on internal resources or industry professionals who cannot creatively exercise their ideas to develop unique solutions to remedy the source of the difficulties. Sometimes businesses need a multi-faceted person to get them to change their perspective and focus differently in order to see unique solutions more clearly.

Judy's organization did not do anything inherently wrong: they searched for a solution within their industry as many businesses will rightfully do in performing their due diligence. However, what too many organizations suffer from is a simple lack of variety in perspectives when dealing with problems and formulating solutions. Where businesses go wrong is not in trying in earnest to fix their problems, it is in failing to get insights from enough perspectives. Variety also brings visibility, which for businesses, is definitely a performance enhancer.

Lesson Eight:
Focus on the Target

One reason why fencing is such a cool sport is the interaction of the weapons upon contact. The clinking and clanking of steel-upon-steel is a pretty neat sound to hear and is exciting to watch. However, the reality is that this interaction is best left for entertainment value as it is not very practical in fencing from a purposeful standpoint.

In many sports such as basketball, football, and hockey there is something known as 'incidental contact' which is contact made as a 'natural' occurrence – which may be by accident or by purpose – but no foul has been committed. Incidental contact occurs in sports when two players brush up against each other as they are running – or skating – past one another and bump each other as is permitted by the sport so long as the contact does not constitute a foul play.

In fencing, incidental blade contact happens as a natural part of the sport. Purposeful blade contact is an inherent component of fencing. An attacking fencer may seek to strike against an opponent's blade to nudge it out of the way first. (This is the first part to a 'beat attack.') A defending fencer has two defensive choices: to parry by weapon or to parry by distance. Additionally, those two methodologies can be combined whereby the defending fencer can parry by using both weapon and increasing the distance between themselves and the attacking fencer. In the attack-parry-riposte choreograph there will be plenty of blade contact that is a natural part of the sport, some of it done on purpose (e.g. by the attacker in posturing for an attack or in testing an opponent's reactions, or by the defender when parrying) and some of it done in the ordinary occurrence of the action as will happen with two steel swords being independently maneuvered.

Beginner fencers – because of their lack of experience – tend to focus on the opponent's weapon, not the target area (e.g. the torso which is a common target area in all three weapons). This is not unexpected: if you were new to sword fighting and someone was challenging you with a sword, and your only exposure to the sport was what you saw in movies and television, you might be focused on clinking-and-clanking the opponent's sword too. (As I tell my beginner students: You don't get points for making more noise.) But this is not actually the target an experienced fencer is truly focused on, at least not me.

The real target of focus is the spot on the opponent's target area where the attacking fencer wants to hit. Notice I said 'the spot' on the opponent's target area, not 'the general area' on the opponent's target area where the attacking fencer wants to hit. When I coach fencing, I instruct my students to focus on the spot where they want to hit. If they get close, that is good enough for me. Hey – even I don't always hit the exact spot I am aiming for, but that does not mean I don't aim for the exact spot I am trying to hit.

In teaching my students to aim for the exact spot they want to hit, I also have to teach them to avoid the obstacles in the way. Or namely, the one significant obstacle in their way: their opponent's weapon. The object of fencing – at least the way I teach the sport – is not to necessarily engage the opponent's weapon, but rather to avoid it during an attack so as to strike at the target spot. Granted, experienced fencers will know this is a somewhat simplistic description as there are maneuvers such as binding-the-blade (taking control of the opponent's weapon) which are quite effective (and fun!) to execute for an attack. Nonetheless, my explanation is accurate: the less engagement with the obstacle in the way when attacking the opponent, the better. By avoiding the obstacle in the way, the weapon, less total effort is required and the attack should be over more quickly. Overall, therefore, it is a more effective and efficient attack. And don't worry: it is still plenty cool to watch from what my fencers tell me of my attacks, even if there isn't as much accompanying noise.

Business execution fails when the organization loses sight of the true target. Obstacles cause distractions, and distractions make it easy to lose sight of the true target. In fencing, an attacking fencer will attempt to distract an opponent through fast motions of the weapon, feinting (faking) a move in one direction whereby the opponent has committed their weapon to that defense and leaving part of their target area open and vulnerable, and then the attacker quickly altering the weapon's trajectory to a new direction with a disengage or coupé and to the opponent's now open target area. Considering the speed at which fencing occurs, this all may happen within the timespan of a second or so. For the attacking fencer, this maneuver avoided the opponent's weapon, the obstruction in the way. For the opponent, the attacking fencer's distraction resulted in a point scored against them.

But business obstacles can sneak up, bubble up, and fester up over the course of weeks and months, if not years. Software system inadequacies may be due to feature failures or data integrity problems that render the information output unable to support strategic decision making. Inefficient operations may be the cause of increased processing time or excessive staffing requirements, the latter of which may also be required to cover for a lack of software or technology tools needed to automate processes and functions. I have witnessed businesses throw six-figures of good money out the window (or down the drain, depending upon your perspective or choice of metaphors) on poorly conceived software projects that did next to nothing to improve business processes and, in some cases, only caused the situations to be worse. Distraction? Disaster!

The target for most companies should be the execution of the Perfect Order. The attributes of the Perfect Order are described in an article I read that is dated February 9, 2005, which describes the customer's bill of rights. However, I believe that this customer bill of rights better defines the characteristics of the execution of the Perfect Order. You can access this article for yourself by going to the web link:

http://www.mhlnews.com/global-supply-chain/customers-bill-rights

To summarize the components of the Perfect Order, (a.k.a. the Customer's Bill of Rights), a company should be delivering:

1. The Right Product.
2. In the Right Quantity.
3. From the Right Source.
4. To the Right Destination.
5. In the Right Condition.
6. At the Right Time.
7. With the Right Documentation.
8. At the Right Cost.

If your company is not able to execute the Perfect Order on a consistently high basis (think back to the sixth level of sigma and do some research on the defect differences between the different levels of sigma), then your company is likely not focusing on the right target. Or maybe your company is not able to focus on the desired target. Or perhaps your company is unable to correctly identify what the right target is, and at each point in the process. If any of these are true, your organization is probably plagued by too many obstacles to be able to focus squarely on what is important which is why it is missing the mark too many times. Are there too many distractions preventing your company from effectively getting to the target? Or was this chapter a revelation as to what the true target of your company should really be?

As this book reveals, you don't attack an opponent in a single, full-on motion. (At least I don't, even though it may look that way due to my speed and experienced technique. As I explain to my students, I deploy the same individual movements I show them, it is just that they are all time-compressed together because I have been fencing for a lot longer than they have, and I am more disciplined at it mentally and physically. I tell my students that they will get to where I am too in a matter of time.) You attack a problem in pieces. The Perfect Order is a description of a business process's individual components.

As NASA (National Aeronautics and Space Administration) is famous for saying: To be off by an inch, is to be off by a million miles. A rocket on Earth that is misdirected by an inch will miss its target by 'a million miles' by the time it travels its path into space. It is a rather simple mathematical concept. (Actually, I think it has more to do with angles.)

In business, flaws and errors early in the process can have a ripple effect and create a greater distortion later on, potentially manifesting themselves into something worse. It is not enough to simply focus on the target. It is critical to understand the process path of getting to the target and ensuring that the technique of the execution is as perfect as possible every time. This helps to guarantee that the scoring touchpoint is on target each and every time. Obstacles are a distraction, and distractions can distort the process and inhibit a fencer's – or a business's – ability to be successful.

Lesson Learned

There are many different types of obstacles that impede the ability to achieve the goal of getting to the target. Misdirections, incorrect perceptions, and clouded clarity are examples of the causes of a failure to focus. Identifying the right target is the first task in the process of the attack. What is the best path to the target? Sometimes the most direct path will not be available to you, so a little detour may be required along the way. Is it better to take on and tackle the obstacles in your path directly, expending energy and effort in doing so, or to avoid the hindrances to the target and reserve precious resources in the sidestep? Essentially, do you want to primarily try and out-muscle – or in business, out-spend – your problems or out-think them and use your resources more wisely?

Lesson Nine: Use What Works First

There are different attack and defense moves in fencing. Different fencers will acclimate more to some moves versus others depending upon their comfort levels and their own styles. Some moves have fewer motions to them, making them characteristically easier to learn and thus realistically better foundational moves to absorb and build upon. The standard parry four and parry six are fairly straightforward defensive moves to execute with minimal motions and the ripostes are rather direct. The parry four is a simpler defensive move than a parry circle-six however, because the circle-six involves an additional motion and more precise timing and distance. The riposte options on the circle-six can require a little more thought. As such, I have found that the circle-six parry is better saved for later on in the lessons due to its slightly more advanced nature. Therefore, I teach my students the simpler parry four and parry six and want my students to become comfortable using them before expecting them to integrate a more complex parry like the circle-six.

The concept of building upon a foundation set of skills, from basic to more advanced, allows the student to experience aspects of fencing in a logical sequence, learning in progression as they go and grow. As much as I want my students to be proficient fencers, I understand that they will probably not gravitate to every attack and defensive maneuver in the proverbial book. It is my job as a coach to present to them a variety of options and let my students choose what works for them, and when. It is also my job as a coach to build upon what works first, given that each student will favor different moves, probably at different times of their development, and as their unique styles of fencing evolve. I don't want to squelch the creativity of my students in their separate development and enjoyment of fencing.

To ensure my students each evolve as effectively as possible while maintaining the enjoyment they have, I build upon what works first on an individual basis. Knowing what foundational maneuvers will realistically work for all fencers, I know where to begin with everyone. From there, some fencers will develop slowly, others more quickly. Some fencers will favor certain advanced moves over others. The essence here is that I can start everyone from the same beginning point and let them grow as individuals, and yet achieve their same objective: to learn how to fence.

In business, for the common objective of perfect operational execution, an organization can start at what works first and grow from there. What works first may be a business model initiative, operational processes, service goal, product line, or use of an existing software system.

For example, before a company tackles the rigors of supply chain technical and operational compliance by attempting to sell to top-level customers in a business-to-business model, it might want to ensure that it can successfully sell direct in a business-to-consumer model.

It is the brass-ring of many budding businesses to sell into retail or grocery, whether brick-and-mortar or online. But even if the business involves a distributor who handles much of the direct customer interface, if the business cannot be successful in manufacturing and logistics to just get their goods to their distributor warehouses, forget about to their own warehouse locations, what makes it think it can take on the direct selling of its products to top-level customers and/or consumers?

When I am approached by up-and-coming businesses who want to take their products to retail, I engage them in a question-and-answer session to determine their level of sale maturity. Do they have an online store right now? Are they currently selling through distribution? Do they sell to any customers direct? Perhaps before considering going to the top-level customers, they would be better off seeking mid-level stores models or kiosk sales (not necessarily their own) first to see if they can be successful there. It could also help build a brand and a following.

Inasmuch as a business needs to invest to continue to advance, I have noticed that businesses tend to fail to get their money's worth out of their investments. It is bad enough that businesses send their employees to training that is not fully utilized on the job. But businesses spend a lot of money on software systems that are either too complicated for what the organization needs, or where the employees are never sufficiently trained on how to use the software to the fullest extent. The end result is that the company was probably better off sticking with what they had in the first place before making rash, hasty buying decisions. Understandably this is a balance: sometimes, especially in software or equipment, what is currently operating may have been used or maintained or abused past the point of practical use.

But before spending money because you think you need new software (for example) or you are unhappy with a business process that is not as efficient as you think it should be, or could be, have you explored the root causes of your dissatisfaction? Before you implemented new software, did you analyze whether the source of your problems was a lack of clean data or data that is conducive to supporting the business in the current state? Were your current employees properly trained on the software? Are your business processes clearly documented and reviewed for efficiency? Starting with what you have before scraping it altogether often builds a better foundation for understanding. Even if you do make some changes, you will be the wiser, understanding the current state first.

Lesson Learned

In fencing, expertise in execution is built upon a foundation of basic skills. These fundamental techniques are based on the knowledge that once the student learns how to perform these simple maneuvers, the more complex routines will be easier to learn, understand, and execute. Not every student will use everything they learn, as each person is unique in what they do and how they do something. This is a person's own style. If a person sticks with using what works first, what comes next will be easier.

For a business, sticking with what they do best will help ensure they produce a quality service or product. The fulfillment of that service or product requires an examination of what resources the organization has and whether the business can use what they have to sufficiently and successfully meet their execution goals. Before jumping into overly complex technology and overly complicated business processes, especially before committing to a market or channel that may be beyond reach, the organization needs to ensure that it can be successful in using what works first because what works next will only be more challenging and have the potential to cause more chaos to the company, and thus disrupt any plans for success.

Business tends to have more resources within their organization than their leaders often realize in terms of software system functionality and personnel capability. How these resources are harnessed, and when, will help to determine the timeliness of expenditures and whether these become worthwhile investments or just needless costs.

Lesson Ten: Be Passionate in Your Pursuit

In fencing, I instruct my students that if they are going to be the attacker, that means that they have to commit fully to the attack. (This is a lead-in to a later lesson.) A fencer cannot be an attacker and not entirely attack. Water is not partially wet. A fencer may withdraw the attack at different stages in the process, but with regards to the commitment and execution of the attack, I expect the attack to be implemented with passion and ferocity at every step taken. This is just like how I execute my attacks, and how I seek to pursue the business goals and objectives for the companies I help.

A new fencer must learn to overcome the fear of failure. If an attack fails – if the attack is successfully defended by the opponent or if the attack misses – the attacking fencer must have the confidence in their defensive skills and recovery to ward off any counter-attack by the opponent. Of course, this is not always the case as a riposte (counter-attack) by the opponent will sometimes score a point. *C'est la vie*. Nonetheless, a fencer cannot, in my opinion, worry about being on the losing end of an attack-parry-riposte or let the fear of failure overcome and compromise the commitment to the attack. To allow this the fencer has already lost the mental aspect of the bout, and thus realistically has lost the battle itself. The attacking fencer believes at the outset that the attack will be successful because it is the right thing to do at the right time.

A business must decide what it is passionate about before it can pursue its goals and fulfill its objectives. For many businesses, the objective of 'make a lot of money' is the apparent primary purpose. But this might be one that employees may find difficult to passionately pursue. 'Fulfill all customer orders accurately and on time' is a much better business goal and one that employees can be enthusiastic about. Surely, it is one that the business's staff can more closely embrace because it is very likely that each and every one of them has, at some point, been a shopper themselves and knows the disappointment of what it is like to not have an order filled accurately or on time.

The result of filling all customer orders accurately and on time is that the company will make a lot of money, with the expected benefit that the employees will earn bonuses for exceeding reasonable benchmarks. A fencer's objective is to win a bout. How? By scoring a greater number of touchpoints before their opponent does: that is the more immediate goal.

Employees that feel more passionate about what they – and the business – are pursuing are more likely to be engaged with the organization and propel it forward. Non-profit organizations tend to employ people who are passionate about what the organization is dedicated to. And according to the Gallup organization, if these employees feel closer to the business, they are more likely to remain. Instilling passion within an organization's people translates to the people being passionate about the organization, and this, in turn, improves the organization's function and execution. But part of this passionate pursuit has got to be about identifying what the target really is. I love money as much as everyone else, but I am not willing to compromise morals, ethics, principles, or quality to get it. Business leaders have to identify to the employees what the real goals are that the organization is in pursuit of. Identifying relatable goals makes the pursuit more personal. In doing so, the employees will be better enabled to identify the true targets, score solid hits, and success will subsequently follow.

Lesson Learned

Business leaders must identify what it is about what their company does that creates a passion. This passion should be closely tied to the delivery of the company's products and services to the customer. The pursuit should be the perfect execution of the fulfillment of the goods and services to the customer, regardless of whether the customer is internal or external to the enterprise. It is then incumbent upon the company's leaders to instill the passion of the pursuit through the organization's employee hierarchy. A worthwhile goal and attainable target are something that employees can feel are within reach, not unlike what a fencer would recognize about an opponent's target area upon approaching within striking distance. Everything else good will come along after if the true target is kept within focus.

A fencer is best not to concentrate on the win (the objective), but instead, the fencer should focus on each scoring touch to target (the goal). In a business, customer satisfaction (the goal) is the result of the excellence in execution (the process) for each and every order (the target). In achieving this, there should be monetary gains. With a clear focus on identifying what the correct target is, the attacker must be passionate in the pursuit of the target. To focus too much on the benefits and not the pursuit (how to get there and achieve it) is to put the cart before the horse, as the saying goes. I don't worry about winning each bout, I focus on scoring each point before my opponent does. The win, therefore, will come naturally.

If you put your passion into the pursuit, the gains and rewards will come. You might not hit the target each and every time, but that is okay. If my passion is high, I can defend and recover and continue on. In business, there are a multitude of variables and forces beyond the organization's control. In fencing, we don't always know how our opponents will react to our attacks. However, just because we don't always know what to expect, this does not mean we should not be passionate in our pursuits and execute to our fullest capabilities all of the time. To not believe in ourselves is to admit failure before we've started, and thus we are doomed to defeat already.

Lesson Eleven: You Become What You Believe

I think that the phrase 'dress for success' has become lost among the more casual nature of many business climates these days. My observation is that people are abusing the ability to dress casually around the office and certainly could be upping their own bar a bit as a reflection of themselves and their workplaces. When I began working for myself in 1996, I always wore a shirt and tie to the offices of the companies I visited to help, as this was how I traditionally dressed in my prior employment career. After a few years, I began to relax my own dress code as 'business casual' became more acceptable and, in hot-and-humid South Florida, more practical. The telltale sign for me was when I stopped by a luxury resort hotel and the Chief Information Officer was wearing a polo shirt in lieu of his signature jacket, shirt, and tie. That told me something about how dress trends were changing. Yet I don't dress down from at least a nice polo shirt and dress slacks, e.g. I don't wear denim jeans to a company unless I am specifically going to be spending the day in the warehouse, and even then, I will more likely wear a pair of khaki pants instead of denims. I definitely think that how you dress sets a mood and a standard and that we are judged accordingly, consciously or not.

If you are a fan of the Renaissance period, Halloween, comic books, or science fiction and have ever gone to a festival or convention or party, your enjoyable escape is made much more complete when you dress up as your favorite character. For just a little while, you are your character as you engage with other fans of fantasy, magic, and mystery in simulation battles, lively dialogs, artistic recreation, and merriment.

I know that most sports have dedicated uniforms, some more noticeable than others, such as football, baseball, and hockey. Some sports uniforms represent really warrior-type contact sports like football and hockey. Other sports uniforms represent nostalgia that are part of the fabric of America, like baseball.

One thing great about fencing is the uniform and how, when you put on the jacket, mask, and glove, and you put a sword in your hand you actually begin to feel like a fencer. I don't think this sounds childish or foolish: I believe that just like with some other sports, when the athletes put their uniforms on, they begin to feel like the players that they are. But even though I am naturally biased: Face it, there is just something cool about fencing. My goodness, it is, after all, sword fighting, and what youngster – and adult – doesn't really want to be a sword fighter at some point in their lives?

Fencing harkens back to the days when men were chivalrous toward women. When gallantry mattered. And unlike many other sports, swordsmanship is carried on through the movies we love the most, from science fiction to romance to history to adventure to comedy. Fencing is more than a sport; it is the essence of what we are when we engage in it. We are pirates, noblemen, outlaws, knights, futuristic fighters, even if just in spirit. All because we put on our fencing uniforms. All because we are fencers.

Senior executives must instill a belief throughout their organizations with the employees in their company. The employees must have confidence in the leadership, must have confidence in the quality of the products and services, and must have confidence in the quality of the company's execution in the delivery of the goods and services to their customers, internal and external. If this happens, the company will become what it believes it is: a great organization.

But this belief cannot be based upon fantasy and fallacy, so this is where there is some divergence from professional and personal livelihood. When we dress up in our costumes, we know we are really not the characters we imagine ourselves to be. However, when we personally suit up in our sports uniforms, we must believe ourselves to be the athletes we know ourselves to be; this helps to boost our performance. In business, employees must 'suit up' (even if business casual) and become the professionals they are, that they need to be, to propel the organization forward in attacking the challenges it will face and combating the forces against it.

Employee attitude can be enhanced by improving employee morale. What is the confidence level of the employees with regard to the company overall? To the company's senior executives and middle management? What is the employee's take on the company's business processes? How do the employees feel about the company's software systems or manufacturing equipment?

It is not enough for senior executives to create a business identity; they must create the correct business character and then ensure the employees embrace that identity. The business's outward identity – that which faces the customers of the business's goods and services – may not really be the internal identity that the employees see in their job roles. A business whose dual-identity is akin to the tragedy-comedy mask of the theater has created an unsustainable persona. Is the business Jekyll to its external stakeholders (customers and suppliers/vendors) and Hyde to its employees?

What is the identity of a company that sells consumer goods? That of a retailer? A vendor? Of a distributor? Or that of an importer? The answer may be one or several of the previously mentioned identities depending upon their business model. The problem is that the company may not be able to correctly identify what type of company it actually is on its own, therefore what type of company it is asking its employees to believe in and therefore to help it become. This misperception failure can be operationally damaging to an organization because it results in a failure to dedicate resources to critical areas of the business that need support.

Lesson Learned

In the April 14, 2020 edition of the Miami Herald newspaper, a judge in Broward County (Florida) had issued a reprimand letter to attorneys for their casual dress and lack of grooming when they appeared via video for online court proceedings during the coronavirus epidemic when social distancing orders were in place. Apparently, attorneys were failing to present themselves in professional appearance and choice of venue (e.g. in their bedrooms or poolside) in the representation of their clients, and the judge was not having any of it. Judges still have to wear their robes as it was noted. Per the article, Knox College environmental psychology professor Francis T. McAndrew explained the connection between how one dresses and how one performs as follows:

'If you look at how you are dressed, that signals something about what you are prepared to do. So, if you're dressed like a slob and you are in your sweat clothes, you're either prepared to work out at the gym or clean out the basement, but you're not doing anything professional or mentally challenging, and that spills over into your motivation and confidence.'

The article concludes with a summary of a popular sports saying: 'You look good, you work good.' But I really like how the article ends, as the judge is quoted stating: 'You're going to earn the same amount of respect that you're shown. If you show up in jeans and a T-shirt, it's counterproductive.'

It is not just enough to want to become a great athlete or a great company, there has to be belief from within that you are that character which you ascribe to be. For an individual, the confidence is personal and the challenge is somewhat singular. A person needs to put themselves into the mindset of the athlete they want to become. Wearing the uniform helps to create the aura of this alternate personality and shift the person into becoming a competitive athlete. It is okay to pretend in costume when the time and place are right. How a person dresses can have an effect on their attitude.

A business is a much more complex entity. Comprised of many people performing different supporting tasks, there are different identities within a business that all go toward creating the common goals and objectives. But these identities can also clash can cause considerable chaos. Business leaders need to understand that these different identities do, and need to, exist. For the business to become what the leaders want it to, the employees need to embrace a belief in the organization as a whole plus in their own more individual-focused departmental areas.

While business leaders may like the analogy of draping the superhero cape uniform accouterment around their hard-working staffers, I do not find that comparison to be very helpful. I will chime in that I find office dress codes to be a little more casual than I believe they should be these days, and that an improvement in professional dress would likely lead to an enhancement in performance. While I am cautious not to judge a person by their appearance, I think it is also true that how one dresses makes an impression, a statement, and can influence one's work performance.

I believe an employee's uniform consists primarily of the superhero toolbelt, whose contents in the modern technology age consist primarily of software programs and infrastructure technologies and policies that either enable or obstruct the employee in the performance of their work. Another important item in the toolbelt is business procedures, whether they are clearly defined and functional or undefined and a chaotic mess. Employee education and training is yet another toolkit necessity that is often not sufficiently included by company management. Not outfitting employees correctly fails to enable them to properly suit-up and believe in the company, allowing it to become what the leaders want it to be.

All of us wear different uniforms in our daily lives, personally and professionally. Some of these uniforms we can pick for ourselves, others are handed to us. For the uniforms that are provided to us, these uniforms must be well-equipped to meet the challenges we will face. But if we don't believe in who we are when we wear the uniforms, no amount of corporate logo accessories will make us become what we believe, because our belief will not exist. The persona change happens from within, influenced from outside. The uniform helps to bring out the essence of who we are, it does not create the essence from nothingness. The creation of the essence has to be done through a system of beliefs, and if the company cannot be successful at this, it will not likely succeed, let alone be successful in the delivery of products and services to the satisfaction of its customers.

Lesson Twelve: Are You the Attacker or the Defender?

I was coaching a fencer who was training with me while on summer break from attending university. The student was already fencing on his university's club team and was showing great progress given that he had less than one year of experience. He wanted to keep up his training through the summer and learn some new skills in the process. I noticed that there was some hesitation in his attacks. I asked him what he was thinking about when we were facing each other in the en garde position, ready to engage each other. My new student told me that he thought about whether to attack or not, which, I informed, is incorrect. The problem, as I prodded, was that he didn't think about if and how he was going to attack until it was too late. In effect, when we were set to engage each other, my opposing student didn't attack: he just hesitated because he was stuck in the decision. His attack timing was off because the decision as to what type of attack to engage, assuming that to attack was the decision, was made too late, after the fencers were already allowed to go at each other.

The decision whether to attack or not to attack – to therefore defend – has to be decided upon first-and-foremost. If to attack, then what type of attack to execute. These decisions must be made before an agreement to fence, or at least before a director in a competition signals the action to commence. Incorrect timing, which is what my student was suffering from, caused him to hesitate, or wait to execute his attack. As I tell my students, there is no waiting in fencing: you are either the attacker or the defender. If you are waiting, your opponent is likely as inexperienced as you are. To use the saying: He who hesitates is lost.

My young student was essentially suffering from what is known in the business world as 'paralysis by analysis.' This is the syndrome where a decision is not made because of over-thinking of the information presented and the options the information provides. Because no decision is ever made, the entity making the decision does nothing. As they are not the attacker, they default to becoming the waiter (By 'waiter' I mean an entity that is waiting – I am not using the word to represent a person who is a server in a restaurant.).

But being stuck in 'paralysis by analysis' and in a waiting state does not necessarily translate to defaulting to being the defender. Worse, being in a waiting state likely means – and in fact meant for my young student – that there was no thought given to the possibility of defending an inbound attack either. So, this paralysis limbo state compounds the problem for the fencer in being neither the attacker nor the defender: the fencer is simply a standing target.

Fencers are constantly calibrating – assessing – their opponents for strengths (to be aware of), weaknesses (to take advantage of), opportunities (such as open areas in which to score), and threats (of attack). (Opponent calibration is discussed in greater detail later in the book.) However, because of the speed at which fencing occurs, and due to the right-of-way rule in foil and sabre, the need to decide one's attack strategy before the action begins is a key factor in successfully scoring. There is absolutely nothing wrong with defending as a strategy as long as one is consciously doing so. I do it all the time in fencing, and I am quite effective at it. I will try and bait the opponent into an attack so I can defend and riposte for the score. The difference is being defensive as an offensive strategy versus being defensive as a protective necessity. Or worse, being forced to be defensive because you were standing there like a deer in headlights and caught between thoughts as to what actions to take, and when to take them.

Organizations can essentially take one of two perspectives to strategic management in how they undertake the planning process with regards to the position by executive leadership. An outward perspective is an aggressive, or attacking, viewpoint whereby the company will utilize its resources to accomplish tasks within hopefully short (relative to the individual task) timelines as it pursues agendas to push the company forward. An inward perspective is a conservative, or defensive, viewpoint whereby the company will conserve its resources and takes a slow-go approach. This might be in a situation where the company has limited resources to spare or seeks to wait out market adjustments. Limited resources include the inability to have a long-horizon perspective such as in the case where the company cannot build projections based upon quality data. Other resource limitations include lack of employee staff skills, low cash-on-hand reserves, software system functionality boundaries, and restricted cash flow due to slow sales or late customer payments.

Lesson Learned

Over-aggressive attackers run the risk of not thinking through their plans and getting out-witted by their opponents who will use their strengths against them. Under-aggressive attackers run the risk of not scoring enough points to win a bout. To always be on the defensive is to always start at a disadvantage, which I would not recommend to any of my students. The graceful balance between when to be the attacker and when to be the defender is in-and-of-itself part of the learned experience in becoming a great fencer.

Businesses must consciously consider when they need to attack the external and internal challenges that are foiling their abilities to reach their targets and execute their organization's plans. Business must also be able to contemplate when it is the right time to take a defensive stance and carefully wait out a situation, letting perhaps another entity (competitor, customer, vendor, the market) move first and set the tempo.

But paralysis by analysis – or its companion, complacency – displays a lack of leadership by executive management in businesses. This will negatively affect an organization's ability to address serious issues affecting its ability to operationally execute and successfully score target touches, namely the accurate fulfillment of goods or services to its customers.

Lesson Thirteen: Distance Adds Perspective

In American football and soccer (otherwise known in Europe as 'football'), which player on the field has the best perspective of the action? In American football, it is the quarterback, and in European football (a.k.a. 'soccer'), it is the goalkeeper. In both of these positions, one beneficial factor in their enhanced perspective of the playing field is in their extra distance from the state of play. These two positions can survey the field and ascertain who is covered, who is about to be covered, who is open, or who is breaking to an open position. Their farther distance from the action is a benefit, not a disadvantage, in their wide perspective of the field.

Inasmuch as there is infighting (close proximity combating) in fencing, I prefer to be at a (relative) distance from my opponent when I battle and execute my attacks and parries. I like my shield – the bell guard – in between me and my opponent. I like my target area at as much distance from my opponent as possible. (In foil, I basically always lunge in my attacks, and that creates a natural distance within the style itself given that my weapon arm is fully extended to my opponent. As such, the distance between my target area – my torso – and my opponent is at least the combined length of my outstretched arm and weapon.) If my attack should fail, I know I can rely on my shield and distance as defensive tools, along with my speed and quick reflexes. More tools in the toolkit. With greater distance, I also have a better perspective of my opponent: their stance, weapon position, and available target area. (Analyzing one's opponent, known as 'calibrating,' is covered later in the book.) I can better plan and execute my attacks and, if they fail, the additional distance provides that extra second or so to recover and mount a defensive maneuver. Distance is an advantage to me, offensively and defensively.

Often times in problem-solving when one is too close to the issue, it is difficult to have an objective perspective of the situation. Subjectivity can cloud one's analysis as it taints how a person is viewing a matter. Not only is an understanding of the problem important, but different viewpoints are really without question a practical necessity. Often times outside-the-industry opinions are valuable because businesses operate more similarly than not across industries, though this opinion is rarely realized by those too close or within the industry themselves, which is a damaging myopic perspective.

I have worked in numerous different industries and have found that, essentially, business is business. The purpose of the common business transactions – sales orders, purchase orders, work orders, invoices, bill of lading, pack list, pick list – does not really change from one industry to another. The primary entities that are involved in a business –

customers, vendors, items, sales representatives – are common across many industries. This is why common business software like Enterprise Resource Planning (ERP) from the same software company can often be used successfully across different industries. Once you step back and look at it, business is just business. But company after company where I have been, from one industry after another, people are just too close to the problems to perceive them openly and generically. Aside from a lack of experience, the belief that only their company or their industry has a particular problem, or that a solution can only be found within a select pool of industry-specific providers is rarely the case anymore. But people still hang on to and cling to this narrow perspective, which is why they and their companies still need to be coached into a better way of seeing and doing things.

Business leaders that find their companies embroiled in disruption, which they themselves may be the cause of, should take the reins and bring in some outside help to ascertain whether the organization is failing to see a bigger or clearer picture due to their tight industry focus. There is nothing wrong with being experts in a particular field, but it is this expertise that sometimes prevents people from understanding that business solutions can be found from outside of their industry. The value benefit is that this outside perspective can pay for itself by recommending solutions that are more functional at a lower investment cost.

The companies I help know their industry, but I tend to know their business with more insight. While the companies I help may have their expertise in their particular industries, I am really the one who sees better their operational, software, and data challenges, can guide them to the solution opportunities, carry them through the project implementations, and lead them forward toward more strategic management and growth by pulling in ideas gleaned from other industry and business engagement experiences.

Lesson Learned

Each and every time I force my fencers to step back away from the attack, they agree that the added distance helps them to see more of their opponent and the entire action. The extra distance enables my students to expend fewer resources in maneuvering their weapons for their attacks, and gives them extra time to recover should an attack have to be withdrawn, or it is defended successfully and the opponent ripostes with a counter-attack. Added distance in fencing is a benefit, not a detriment.

More distance adds perspective. Sometimes, you need to step back to see a problem more clearly. Your perception of the issue may have been tainted until you have stepped away and taken a different perspective, able to see more of the situation which changed your opinion of the circumstances. With the renewed clarity comes a better chance at identifying the true target or the real root cause, and then coming up with the right attack plan to score a winning hit. If you cannot take this step away by yourself, get a coach to help you.

Lesson Fourteen: Patience Is a Virtue... And a Pain in the Pants

I am regularly asked by new fencers, or their parents if they are youngsters, when do I believe they will be ready to compete in a competition. I caution my inquisitors that they are too new to something they have never done before, and that to be skilled in something takes time. I also warn them that they will be going up against people – and this includes other children – who will be more experienced and will be taking the competitive nature of this very seriously. (Competitions do not pair children against adults. Fencers are separated by age groups.) Essentially, even if just figuratively as I would hope it would never be literally, I express to my new students and their parents that their opposition may be out for blood. So, if they are not well-prepared physically and mentally, if their skills are not well-developed, they may want to wait a while. How long is 'a while' depends upon each unique individual person, of course. And after we have this little chat, they are less likely to jump head-first into a competition. It is not that I purposefully want to discourage them from testing their mettle or metal, but there is a right time for everything. Diving head-first into a competition might personally dishearten a new student and dissuade them from continuing their lessons and pursuing something that they enjoy doing.

Inasmuch as companies need to work at the proverbial speed of business and execute rapidly to meet their customer demands and market changes and challenges, it is also true that hastily made decisions cost companies more money than well-thought-out conclusions. Improvements take time as well as resources. If the company is not willing to allocate both, then there is likely little point to the project. Even a 'natural born' or prodigy fencer is a rarity at the very best, the reality being that time is required to hone one's skills through training, practice, and instruction.

There is much to be learned by a new fencer from engaging in their first competition, as long as the expectation is set from the beginning. The excitement of participating on 'the big stage' can be enticing but also unsettling. No matter the size of the competition, it can give a person butterflies in their stomach to have a bunch of strangers, let alone friends and family, watching you do something for the first time and judge your performance. This adds to the pressure of the competition. It is not much different a feeling perhaps than for first-time public speakers who might already be a little socially shy. The eyes of the audience are upon you, yet your focus needs to be on your skills and the challenge that lies immediately before you.

Learning how to quickly adapt to fencing against complete strangers is another competition benefit and complication. Fencers tend to get into a rhythm when they fence against known opponents as the expectation of each opponent's style become recognized. However, being challenged by a previously unopposed adversary requires a fencer to analyze even quicker, ascertaining the opponent's strengths and weaknesses sooner so that the opportunities for scoring and the threats of attack can be more quickly identified. Remember: not only is fencing a very fast sport, but initial elimination bouts are typically only five-point matches, so there is not much competitive margin for error.

While it may seem counter-intuitive that a fencer cannot have patience in a competition, nothing is further from the truth. The patience a fencer has is embedded within the technique. As I tell my students, it may look like I am executing a maneuver all at once, but in fact, I am executing a series of multiple motions in rapid-fire sequence. Each motion is simply time-compressed from one move to the next move because I have been doing this for so very long (over 25 years) and it is through experience, physical fitness, and mental training that I am able to execute with such speed and accuracy the multiple steps within a maneuver, especially true in an attack or riposte counter-attack. But the point here is that the maneuvers are multiple moves, and at any point, within the maneuver, I can make a change. There is, embedded within my process, patience mixed with swiftness and decision-making.

I have witnessed businesses who have blown through tens of thousands, hundreds of thousands, and millions of dollars forgetting that it is critically important to mix patience with fleetness. That a full-force attack is not a huge, singular execution but a series of individual motions that are executed individually in ideally rapid succession but with the option of embedding patience at each point if a change needs to be made. A change may be a sudden stop or an alteration in direction.

Consider that part the mastery behind world-renowned systems of quality is the theory that at any time a worker on the assembly line can halt the process due to a quality defect rather than letting the defect continue on and possibly manifest into something potentially worse. As rapidly as the assembly process needs to move, if a quality problem occurs the process stops, the problem is found, the defect cause is resolved, and then the assembly line is allowed to restart. Defects are not detected at the end, nor do they end up in the customer's hands, but rather during the process which is where any alterations are made to ensure a successful outcome.

Remember: fencing moves (e.g. an attack, a parry-riposte combination) are the accumulation of smaller, individual motions that in aggregate make up the entire maneuver. In between each motion, the fencer has the option of a decision to make which will affect the next motion's execution: to proceed to the next motion, to stop the maneuver altogether, or to alter how the next motion is going to be executed from the original plan. The fencer has little more time than the blink of an eye in which to decide this and execute the decision and follow-up motion which includes a stop.

In business, the dividing-and-conquering of a larger job into much smaller tasks is generally known as project management. In each phase of a project, the individual steps are identified. In a project, there may have to be alterations to how the project proceeds based on uncontrollable factors that influence the organization, just like a fencer reacting to their opponent. Is your company one that has a history of successful projects, on time and on budget? If not, why? Did you attack your problems by embedding patience into the project, or did you just throw yourself at it full-on?

Lesson Learned

We all want to get there as soon as possible, but there is a price to be paid for pushing it. Embedding patience in a process does not slow it down. Rather, it ensures that there are always options available when new challenges are encountered as will always be the case. Companies do not always have control over the forces they are competing against, in the same way, that a fencer has minimal, if any, real control over their competitor. Changing market forces, personnel resources, and software system issues are the typical challenges that can occur during a business project that will always be wrapped within budgetary and timeframe constraints. Patience provides the agility to sidestep the roadblocks to success. But the organization has to be able to overcome its own political and prideful agendas which are likely bigger barriers inhibiting its ability to be successful. This points back to company culture.

Fencers who rush to complete their attacks believe that they are accomplishing something, when all that they are doing is exhausting themselves. This takes us back to the previous lesson in the book of the balance between the process and the results: both are important. When I see a fencing student continually failing to touch target and score points after repeated failed attack attempts, I stop and we analyze what is going wrong. If I am defending too easily with my weapon, my student is probably rushing their attacks and is too focused on the target and not enough on the process. If I am defending too easily with distance, either out of distance or the student is missing me easily (the student's weapon is constantly going past me or falling short), the student is likely focused too much on the process and not enough on the resultant target spot. By forcing the student to reset and rethink, I get them to achieve the balance and discipline they need.

Businesses cannot be so impatient that they place the priority on the process (project successes) over the results (the product the project was intended to deliver), or visa-versa, lest the company risks creating final products – which may miss the mark – based upon unsubstantiated analysis. Being patient is not a cost, it is an investment. Because when it is the right time to attack, you will be able to do so with confidence that it is the right decision at the right time. I would rather score on the first attack attempt than have to repeatedly try and try again, running the risk of frustration and using up valuable resources.

Lesson Fifteen: Problem Solving Using Versatile Viewpoints

As I have already recounted, my fencing skills had plateaued until I began assisting my former fencing coach as an instructor. The fact was that we had an abundance of students and I did not want any of them to feel like they were not getting their money's worth for their time at the old club. As it is my nature, I leaped in to help ensure the club – which was not mine at the time – was providing quality customer service. As a result, I actually benefitted as much as the students I was providing training to. By helping the students learn what they were doing incorrectly and explaining the proper techniques of the attacks and defenses (and footwork), I began to realize what I was not doing correctly myself. It became an introspective perspective that was enabled first by outward examination.

Teaching gives you this alternate viewpoint over more than just than participating. I use this lesson to this day, getting my fencers involved surprisingly early in their education as I deputize them into being 'explainers,' if not 'instructors,' to other fencers of if nothing more than just footwork and the most very basic of weapon maneuvers. This forces even the newer fencers to focus on the technique as they describe the proper method of performing the weapon or footwork skill. My students become quicker learners as well and have greater confidence in their skills because they understand the inner workings of what I am instructing them to do. This higher level of comprehension makes them more decisive fencers, giving them the ability to act and react to challenges quicker as they learn. It also enhances the social aspect of the fencing club, which goes along with the culture I seek to establish.

In business, leaders who do not understand the nature of the tasks their staff employees are engaged in performing suffer an understanding gap, which creates an issue when it comes to solving execution problems. How can business leaders accurately determine the cause of execution problems if they cannot perceive the problems their organization staff is suffering from alternate perspectives? The staff employees are likely to perceive their problems from a singular perspective. Are the problems personnel-related, e.g. a bad employee (attitude, poor training)? If so, who? The employee complaining, or another employee in the mix?

Is the problem related to poor business procedures? Are there any procedures documented and, if so, are the documented operating procedures well organized? Are the operating procedures that are documented an accurate and up-to-date reflection of what is actually occurring within the organization?

Is the problem related to software, either a system that is in use or the lack of a software system? If the problem is related to an in-use software system, was there sufficient training on that system for the employees? Was that training included in the updated business operating procedures? Is the data in the software conducive to the business needs? If the problem is related to a lack of supporting software, are the employees suffering from shuffling manual or electronic paper (e.g. spreadsheets or document files)? Are employees forced to create spreadsheets to compensate for the lack of any other software to manage some data, and is their problem compounded by the fact that they are not skilled in spreadsheet design and management?

Is the problem a perception difference between employees with different roles? The typical example is how the people in the information technology area view a problem versus how the people in the business operations departments view the same problem.

If the business leader is too far separated from the staff to perceive the various problem viewpoints and get to a root-cause analysis, the organization needs to assign a qualified analytical person to assist in this inquiry. A middle manager would be an appropriate person to get involved in the investigation, but may not be the best person to examine the execution challenges given that the problems may be operational, software, personnel, or a combination. The middle manager may not have the sufficient time to handle the investigatory analysis.

Placing yourself in an alternate perspective is one useful technique to solving a problem. Another useful method of problem-solving is to consider alternate solutions from outside of the obvious. Often times, businesses believe that solutions to their problems can only be found within their industry. However, I have found this to be more often incorrect than true. Software is an especially relevant example of a business tool that can be utilized generically across a variety of industries.

Businesses waste considerable time and money by not thinking from versatile viewpoints. The result is higher project costs, extended project timelines, more disruption to the business, the inability to overcome challenges, and failures to execute plans, accomplish goals, meet objectives, and satisfy customer requirements.

Lesson Learned

For some people, there is no better way to learn than to do. But paraphrasing the saying, there is also likely no better way to learn than to teach. Combining the two together truly forges the ability to learn 'how' to do something and the 'why' of that something. I don't think you can have one without the other as a participant and be successful.

In business, the ability to solve problems successfully requires people who understand the 'how' and the 'why' and the 'what' to analyze the situation and can use a versatile perspective to see through the chaos and establish the source of the disruption. Businesses need critical thinkers with varied experiences who can leverage their backgrounds to creatively solve problems and get their organizations back on the track to execution. It is up to the senior leaders to ensure their companies either develop these skills in-house or have access to these talents on the outside as needed. Indecision as a viewpoint is an execution-killer in any organization.

Not in a dissimilar way to what happens in my fencing club as I pass along my knowledge and insights of the sport to my students, the establishment of perspective teams within a business can take on the mentor-protégé relationship. These internal partnerships can be career-enhancing experiences for both parties, help to bridge generational and viewpoint gaps, and yield great benefits when it comes to project success.

Lesson Sixteen: Calibrating Your Opponent

In fencing – which is a one-on-one combat sport – there is something called 'calibrating' your opponent. This is where a fencer analyzes the opponent's capabilities and weaknesses. The calibration of one's opponent typically happens during the fencing bout, what I would call 'active calibration,' but can also occur passively, (what I would term 'passive calibration') such as when one fencer is a non-participant in a bout and watching another fencer who is a participant in a bout. This passive calibration is typical at competitions when fencers have advance notice of who they are going to be fencing, but also occurs at my club when one resting fencer observes other fencers practicing and contending against each other.

What does a fencer need to know about their opponent? I can summarize that in the following way:

- **Strengths**: What attack moves does the opponent like to utilize? What are the opponent's preferred parry (defensive) moves?

- **Weaknesses**: Does the opponent tend to favor one parry option over another? What attacks does the opponent generally not execute? Is the opponent slower than I am? Does the opponent have a shorter reach than I do? What maneuvers does the opponent not utilize?

- **Opportunities**: Does the opponent generally leave a particular area of target vulnerable? Can I work my way inside the opponent's reach? Can I use my greater speed against the opponent? Does the opponent have a particular 'tell' or signal or visual indicator that is a warning of an attack?

- **Threats**: Can the opponent outreach me? Is the opponent faster than me? Does the opponent execute an attack maneuver I am not familiar with or cannot counteract (parry/defend against) effectively? Is the opponent an opposite-handed fencer? (This can present a unique challenge.)

For the knowledgeable business folks reading this book, the above was purposefully summarized into a SWOT analysis, and that was the point. This accurately describes what a fencer does in calibrating their opponent, and the SWOT analysis is what a business does in analyzing its opponents, namely its competitors.

When I calibrate my opponents in fencing, this does not mean that I shy away from them in a bout. Quite the contrary: it simply means that I understand my opponents and their capabilities. Yes, it often does mean that I acquire this understanding on-the-fly, but at least I obtain and can use this knowledge when I need it the most which is during a fencing bout.

Knowing who my competition is and what they are able to do – and not do – well allows me to adjust and fine-tune my methodology. I don't change my style just because of my opponent; rather, I may alter my strategy of the attacks I choose, the parries I use, or the ripostes I select. I stay true to myself and my style of fencing and work within the skillset that I have. I try to force my opponent to play my game, just as I know my opponent is trying to force me to play their game.

In fencing, I also calibrate myself: I know who I am as a fencer and what I am capable of offensively and defensively. I know my favorite bread-and-butter moves. I know my out-of-the-hat trick moves. I know my visual giveaway clues, so sometimes I do them with follow-up and sometimes I do them without follow-up. I also know what moves I just don't do, and that is okay too.

Before a business does a SWOT analysis of their competition, they should perform one of themselves. This is sure to be an introspective perspective that is going to be – needs to be – a brutally honest look in the mirror about the capabilities and functionalities of the organization. It is unlikely to be an objective examination the business is able to undertake on its own: a third-party or outside viewpoint will likely be required to help assess the actual state of the organization's strengths, weaknesses, opportunities, and threats to itself before it considers those that are external. An entity must understand itself and its place among its customers, suppliers/vendors, competitors, and the marketplace before it can challenge the opponents and forces it will face.

Lesson Learned

My assumption when I face off against a fencing opponent, especially one that I have never been challenged by before, is that they are at least as capable a fencer as I am. If I have to set the bar somewhere, I would rather set the bar high rather than start out with the bar low. I believe that in calibrating one's opponent it is important to not start from nowhere, but rather to begin at a starting point. It is my opinion that a better starting point is one of equivalency rather than of dominancy with regard to mine and my opponent's. It keeps me on guard so I am better prepared for what my opponent may actually show skill-wise. It allows me to stay confident and cautious.

In business, when I encounter a new company and its representatives in our introductory meeting, my assumption is that they know what I know. This is typically not entirely true, or else we would not be meeting at all. Nevertheless, I assume that they obviously have at least some knowledge of what we are going to talk about, so I give my audience the benefit of the doubt until I understand their level of comprehension about the topics we are discussing, which are technical and operational areas of disruption and opportunity within their business. Inasmuch as these people – as representatives of their company – are not my competitors, it is important that I calibrate their individual responsibilities and positions within the organization and how they interact with and affect or are affected by the situation we are discussing. I need some starting point from where to begin my assessment of the company's problems, and I have found this to be a good place to commence when it comes to first meetings. I am, after all, there to help.

Performing an analysis of one's position, whether as an individual in a situation, an employee in a company, or as a business entity in a corporate marketplace, is a fundamental technique that I believe is critical to be able to perform. I maintain that until one understands what their own true position is relative to the others they are engaged with within the immediate and larger environment, they cannot truly determine how to effectively use the skills they have, and the opportunities presented to them, to successfully compete against challengers and succeed against competitors. Reflective internal and analytical outward calibration – done via a SWOT analysis – is an essential technique that has applicability to both sport and business.

Lesson Seventeen: Use Your Opponent's Strengths Against Them

Fencing is not about forcing the opponent's weapon to your will. Fencing is primarily about avoiding the opponent's weapon as you maneuver your weapon through the opponent's open area toward the opponent's target area. As I have already explained, there is incidental blade contact that happens in fencing, as there is incidental contact that happens in many other sports. Also true in fencing, there is purposeful blade contact during attacks as in the beat attack where an attacking fencer will strike a beat against an opponent's blade before executing a follow-up motion, e.g. the disengage underneath circular movement. The purpose of the initial beat is to cause the opponent's weapon to shift suddenly out of the current position. The opponent will then rapidly attempt to reposition their weapon which will leave them vulnerable and open to one of several possible follow-up attacking moves, e.g. a direct lunge or a disengage by the challenging fencer. The beat attack is a calculated leverage move when done correctly: the attacking fencer performs the beat with a stronger part of their weapon against a weaker part of the opponent's weapon.

In the grand scheme of things with regards to the attack-parry-riposte repertoire that occurs within fencing, the overall strategy is not to leverage and hold an opponent's weapon. There is a maneuver technique where binding or controlling an opponent's blade in a momentary circular movement has a brief advantage. However, if circled for too long, this maneuver can backfire as the opponent can charge through and effect a scoring touch. This can happen when the fencer who has taken control of the opponent's blade in the binding circle actually brings the opponent's blade around in the circular motion to the fencer's target area. If the opponent is quick enough to escape the speed of the binding circular motion, the fencer who thought they were in control can be scored upon. This is a neat maneuver by the fencer in control when executed properly and released just at the correct time; otherwise, it is just embarrassing to bring the opponent's weapon into scoring position. Inasmuch as what I just described happens more in foil, even in sabre, where the fencers tend to go at each other like mountain rams battering each other with their horns, there is still an element of obstacle avoidance in how I teach the sabre attack: in pushing the weapon forward, the attacking fencer makes contact with the opponent's weapon at the bell guard, or captures the opponent's weapon by controlling the blade, and then completes the attack motion by closing upon the target area with the wrist. The obstacle – the opponent's weapon – is encountered as either incidental or purposeful contact but used as leverage and the attack motion completed by the attacking fencer's bend of the wrist as the attacking fencer closes upon the opponent's target area. (More on the use touch and sound as additional resources in fencing coming up soon.) Fencing is really about avoiding (as in foil) or going around (as in sabre) the obstacle – the opponent's weapon – that is blocking the goal: the ability to score a touchpoint on the opponent's target area. Holding on to the opponent's blade for too long does not accomplish the end result: the scoring touch.

When an opponent tries to hold my blade and leverage strength against me, I let them. Physics plays an amazingly prominent role in fencing. As the opponent is leveraging strength against me, why fight it? I could, but it serves no purpose for me. It will simply cause me to needlessly expend energy I could use elsewhere. So, when an opponent wants to leverage strength against me, I momentarily let them until it is to my advantage to break away quickly. My opponent's leveraged strength causes my opponent to have momentum in the direction that they were pushing, and my sudden break-away causes them to continue in that direction, only much more quickly if just for a brief moment. That is usually all the time I need to maneuver the point of my weapon to the exposed area my opponent left wide open by over-committing all that strength to a singular direction, allowing me to score more often than not. For the fencers in my club who have experienced this with me, my reputation as someone who uses their opponent's strengths against them is well established.

In business, for competitors that offer a similar product or service, these companies have to find a way to distinguish themselves from the others and can look to their opponent's strengths to determine how to leverage those apparent assets against them. Your competitor may be a larger company than yours, but perhaps its customer service is not very effective, e.g. limited hours of service. Your competitor may not offer very good touchpoints through email for online orders. Maybe you could offer a better return policy. Or perhaps you could slip free inexpensive trinkets or promotional items in with every shipped order, just as an extra way of saying 'thank you.'

As someone into his 25th year of being self-employed, I seek ways in which I can use my opponent's strengths against them. For me, even though they are not really competitors due to their massive national and international size and scale, I look at the business models of some top-tier consulting firms and ask myself how I should model my services or image in comparison. Naturally, I don't have the financial resources or bandwidth, strengths a massively large company would have. But, being such a big company, they would also be likely slow to change or respond quickly to an innovative idea that might have to go through multiple committees, whereas I just need to have a thoughtful conversation with myself.

Consider that my first two books are each the first exclusive books on the planet on their respective topics of supply chain fraud and supply chain vendor compliance. I did not invent those topics, I just wrote the first (and only, to date) books ever on those topics. Who did I beat? Everybody! Everyone who works for every accounting firm, audit firm, retailer, supplier, vendor, agency, association, organization, consulting firm, think tank, and university. I beat them all to the punch. Me. A company of one. They are all bigger organizations than I am, but in some ways, I think that is also sometimes their weakness.

Lesson Learned

Businesses may believe themselves to be at a disadvantage against their market competition, but sometimes this is merely a perception misconception. Look again at your competition and understand what your company can do better than they can do because of who they are. Perhaps because your competitor is, in fact, such a monolithic organization that they are slower to innovate, or take longer to make decisions because they have a deeper corporate hierarchy than your company does. Perhaps they have more software systems that need to be linked together, and thus they take longer to aggregate data to formulate meaningful information. Maybe they are not hiring people who are permitted to think as freely or express their creative ideas so readily. Ah, so suddenly their size and strength are not such the advantages as you previously perceived it to be. Superior execution in business is not always linked to size and strength. As previously discussed, what does a SWOT analysis really reveal about your organization and about your competitors, and how can you use your opponent's strengths to your competitive advantage?

Lesson Eighteen: Waste Not

Lean Six Sigma is not just about the continual pursuit of improvement: it is also about removing waste from processes. Unnecessary motions are costly and needlessly consume resources. Double-data entry, manual checking and correction, printing and scanning to electronically store and archive digital information, and excessive communications due to a failure to express oneself (typical when email or text message is used in lieu of just picking up the telephone or have a face-to-face chat) are examples of time-wasting activities that drag down the productivity of business organizations every minute of every hour of every workday. Why don't workers sometimes feel like they get anything done at the end of an arduous day at the office? Well, it is because they probably didn't. Billions and trillions of dollars of technology later, and things seem to be more complicated to accomplish, not less.

In fencing, there are realistically no wasted moves. One reason is likely because the sport is so fast-moving that there is really no time to include a non-productive motion in an attack or a parry. This is not to state that a feint move is not useful, it is, for the purposes of attempting to have the opponent commit or over-compensate their weapon and open a potential area to target. I do not consider a feint move to be wasteful at all; rather, it is quite strategic.

But extraneous motions that have no real purpose are not that much use in fencing. They merely take extra time and effort to execute. Worse, these extra wasteful actions tend to leave the fencer vulnerable to attack by the opponent. So, the waste is not just harmful in that it is consuming resources (energy and time), it is detrimental in that it is leaving the fencer usually unwittingly open to being scored upon. As a fencer, I would take advantage of an opponent who left themselves exposed in this manner and adjust my attacks accordingly. In addition, I would presume that the extra motions would cause the fencer to consume more energy and thus tire more quickly, and I would analyze how I could also take advantage of this possible evolving condition. One way, for example, would be to force the opposing fencer to move up and down the strip (piste) more often, burning even more energy and reducing their stamina level. This should also result in increasing the opponent's frustration level and cause my rival to make more mistakes.

In business, the losses in productivity spreading across the organization may simply be an underlying emotion of perpetual frustration that, after a while, is almost like a white noise in the background that a person becomes apathetic to even though it is still there. But the problem is that the wasteful activities remain present, sucking the efficiencies out of the organization, negatively affecting execution, driving up the costs of conducting business, and continuing to have a damaging effect upon the employees.

Just because something cannot be seen or heard does not mean it is not present and that it cannot cause harm.

Lesson Learned

As I coach fencing, my students will query me as to the movements within a maneuver, asking the 'why' and the 'how' and occasionally being creative in incorporating an extra step they think is necessary. I explain to them how the wasteful motion is actually detrimental to the overall action and can leave them open to being scored upon. As they understand the individual steps within the total process, it becomes apparent to them why the wasteful move is not necessary. This is the key to their understanding: we walk through the process step-by-step.

In business, removing waste from operational processes begins with a thorough examination and understanding of what is trying to be accomplished, and documenting what is the current state of affairs. Then by investigating why things are the way they are, looking into what tools (e.g. software systems) are currently available or are attainable, and ensuring that people have the skills and training that they need, the organization can begin to remove the inefficiencies that are pecking it to death and achieve the streamlined processes which will allow it to reach its operational goals and successfully execute to the full satisfaction of its internal and external customers. Inasmuch as reaching ultimate efficiency may be a utopian fantasy for some companies, the pursuit of perfection remains a worthwhile endeavor, albeit from a practical standpoint, as long as it is balanced with the returns on the investment.

Lesson Nineteen: Using All of Your Resources Resourcefully

People question me if they can be good – or great – fencers because they are concerned about some aspect of their particular physique, e.g. they are short, stocky, slow, lanky. Essentially, in their eyes, they are not perfect physical forms (whatever that is) and thus they do not have confidence in the abilities that they do have in themselves, but are more disturbed about the attributes that they seem to lack. So, my answer is: Why not? There is no reason why each of my fencers cannot be good, or great.

Now, in qualification, there is realistically no chance that anyone from my fencing club (yours truly included) is going on to fence in the Olympics, though I still hold out hope and 'never say never.' It is not that I don't have confidence in my fencers, but I am realistic in my hopes of finding the prodigy. If I do, I am probably buying a lottery ticket that same day. Nonetheless, knowing that I have had younger fencers move onward and participate on their university club teams – a realistic goal – there is certainly no reason why any of my fencers cannot achieve the same competitive result, or perchance greater. What I help my fencers realize are their strengths, what they each have that they are particularly good at utilizing. For some fencers, it is their speed; for other fencers, it is their reach. I help each fencer play to their strengths and understand their weaknesses. We focus on both so that we can perfect what they are good at and improve what they need to work on.

Part of helping my fencers achieve their individual success is teaching them to use not just their strengths – be it their speed or their reach – but also their senses. Sight, touch, and sound play critically important roles in the sport of fencing. The role of the sense of sight is quite obvious: two competitors with swords are battling each other, trying to score against each other's target area. The speed at which fencing occurs requires fast reflexes and hand-eye coordination. Inasmuch as my attacks are very much consciously thought through moves, oftentimes, my parries are subconscious reactions because of the speed of the action and the fact that I am seeing just what I need to see in my opponent's weapon motion in order to react. I also use my peripheral vision a lot: just because a particular aspect of something my opponent is doing – whether it be their body stance, footwork, distance, or vulnerable target area – is not in my primary focus does not mean that I am not aware of it too.

Touch and sound are less obvious senses to use in fencing, but they play very important roles. Touch and sound are great indicators as to whether contact between my blade and my opponent's blade has been made. Depending on the maneuver being executed at the time – and whether

I am the lead fencer in the execution of the maneuver (e.g. I am the attacker or the defender) – either the presence or absence of touch and sound are critically important to me. There are times when I want contact with the opponent's weapon, other times when I don't want contact or it is not necessary for the successful execution of the move. When it comes to touch, I am well-aware of how my feet are in contact with the floor as I shift my mental focus to my footwork in preparation for an attack (typically a lunge) or a quick reverse. The point here is that the senses of touch and sound are additional resources that I engage to enhance my overall capabilities. I teach my students to utilize touch and sound to likewise benefit their fencing abilities. And why not? Aside from enhancing performance, these resources are free, so might as well use them.

In business, problem-solving should seek to first utilize the resources the organization has at-the-ready because few companies can simply spend money without bounds, let alone in a crisis have everything that is needed on-hand. Business resources include software systems, data, suppliers/vendors, inventory (raw materials, components, finished goods), and the talents of their employees, contractors, and consultants. What too many businesses fail to realize are the resources that they have to work with. Resource misuse is another common business problem. Software systems may not be utilized to their fullest extent due to poor data setup or a failure to understand their complete functionality. People can be misused when the company does not understand their background education and experience and assigns them to tasks inappropriate for their skills set, e.g. either beneath their talent level, too far above their talent level (and beyond the point of just being a challenging exercise), or too far outside of their talent set.

Businesses tend to want the shiniest new toys (e.g. software systems and technology) but are ill-equipped to adequately function with them due to a failure to fully understand the effort to correctly implement, deploy across the organization, and have staff trained to utilize the resources to their fullest extent thus reaping the maximum benefit for the investment. Granted, this is a tricky balance because companies can suffer operationally on antiquated software systems or equipment that are detrimental to the organization's ability to successfully execute for the end customer perfectly. However, if the business has not fully investigated the resources it has in the current state, it may be spending needlessly when waiting until it is operationally prudent, growing revenue, and saving for a proper project would be more advisable.

Lesson Learned

There are more resources to be used in fencing than the sword: there is the fencer itself. The physical resources are more than just the obvious physique of the fencer like the fencer's reach, but also include senses that most fencers have: sight, touch, and hearing. The fencer that can skillfully harness their senses has an added advantage over the opponent and will become more attuned with themselves as a competitive athlete and with the intricacies of competition.

(Author's note: For readers who believe that a fencer's reach is an end-all asset, I teach my fencers how to use their weapons, speed, and closing of distance to get inside the reach of their longer-armed opponents. Here, distance – closer proximity – is used as a defensive measure and aggressive action versus defending by distance and being out of reach of an attack.)

Businesses should carefully examine the resources at their disposal before it considers how it spends its money. Is the organization fully utilizing an existing resource? Can it repurpose a resource? Is it missing a key, critical resource? Is the business too resource-heavy in certain areas? Or is the business incorrectly resourced somewhere? Resources here can refer to people, software, equipment, machinery, and suppliers/vendors.

Lesson Twenty: Execution Is Part of Your Brand

How do I know if I am a good fencing coach or not? After all, I am not certified as I have mentioned before. Does certification matter as to the quality of fencing coaching that I am providing? Should it make a difference because my club is a hobby and not my profession? Do I compromise on quality because my club is not my livelihood? The answers to the last three questions above are: No, No, and No.

With regards to how do I know if I am a good fencing coach or not, I let my execution of my instructional duties provide the answer. When a new participant joins the club and one or several of my fencers tells them how well they will learn from me if they pay attention and listen to what I train them on, I know I am providing quality coaching. When the parent of a child who I am coaching exclaims to the parent of a new child student how wonderful and patient I am with their youngster, I know I am providing quality coaching.

When I was a university adjunct instructor, the positive feedback and high marks I received from my students each school term during my four years were the indication that I was providing quality upper-level education. Even students who got into trouble and suffered the penalty for doing so – I never failed to catch the perpetrators who were cheating – gave me high marks for my teaching style.

I have developed my coaching methodology based on my being a logical, analytical, critical-thinking person. My process is set upon the foundation of building upon the basics and is in whole based upon the methods I reveal in this book. Part of the process includes involving the students in an explanation of the 'whys' and the 'hows' of everything. Clear communication is the key to understanding and doing. Similarly, I developed my own teaching style and process at the university. It took me a couple of terms to get settled in. But once I was comfortable and understood the flexibility I had in the classroom to teach the subjects in my own way, as long as I stayed within the guidelines, I made some alterations that improved the learning process for the students, and their survey comments were a reflection of that.

In business the lack of clear communication – whether due to poor documentation of a business process, insufficient or ineffective training, laziness in sending poorly worded emails versus picking up the telephone or getting up and meeting with someone face-to-face, or failing to establish a meeting agenda and define the purpose for the assembly – is a bad behavior characteristic and a key cause of chaos, leading to high operating costs and execution failures. A lack of clear communication can extend to a misinterpretation of data too, which can result in bad decisions being mistakenly made. Companies need to ensure they communicate clearly internally within themselves, and also to their external stakeholders, e.g. customers and suppliers/vendors. If the sales and marketing team promises something, the operations and technology departments had better make certain they can back up that promise. Before the sales and marketing department says something publicly or commits to customer execution, they should check with the rest of the organization.

When the Vice President of Finance from a business I was helping said to me – twice in a two-week period – "Norman, you are worth every penny we pay you," that much-appreciated communication was a reflection upon my professional brand. When the Vice President of Operations from another business I was helping said to me, "Norman, you have really raised the bar of the Information Technology department's performance," that reflected how I execute what I do as a business professional. These comments showcase what no certification in the world can credential, and tell me all I need to know about how well I am doing in the eyes of my professional business peers.

Lesson Learned

How a person or an organization executes what they do is a big part of their brand. Marketing visibility will only be able to get your organization onto the public's radar, but this is not just the beginning and end of your brand. Your brand is part of what is communicated through your performance with your customers. Your brand includes the quality of your product or service, how you deliver it, and how you handle problems with it. You may have a better product or service than your competitors, but if your company cannot deliver it effectively and your competitors can, your company will likely lose the business battle. If your reputation is negative, in the modern era of social media, bad news travels faster and in more abundance than good news, and the word will get out and spread. Quality products and services are almost a commodity nowadays. Execution is the new competitive edge, and your organization better be able to out-perform your competitors in both standard and untraditional ways in order to keep customers happy and win new consumers. It is only through excelling in execution that a fencer wins a bout, and it is only through excelling in execution that a business organization can win, retain, and acquire customers.

Lesson Twenty-One:
Consistency Counts

Inasmuch as it is important to celebrate the wins, in my opinion what matters most in achieving excellence in learning a sport like fencing is to be consistent in execution. This is accomplished through continued training and education. Remember that I believe it is important for my students to think like fencers and understand the 'how' and 'why' of the action. For beginner fencers, I instruct them to practice their footwork and the lunge at home for about 20 minutes most days of the week for the first several weeks, if not first month or two. This enables them to get a feel for their own particular body stance, begin to enhance and strengthen some muscles that they have realistically never used before, and develop a sensation of balance. With this repetitive training comes muscle memory and, as I explain to my students, self-awareness when they are out of proper position as what commonly happens with new fencers who turn in and angle their front foot as opposed to keeping it pointed straight out in the forward direction.

Starting with foundational concepts, getting my students to practice them at home, and building upon the basics, allows my students to quickly become consistent in their skills. It does little good to master the moment if, in fact, the moment is fleeting and is not repeatable. While it is nice to celebrate the score, for example, if it is the only one a student ever achieves in a bout, that is no good. I need my students to be able to repeatedly touch target area and repetitively score points if they are to win duels. Conversely, only parrying one inbound attack ever will result in endless points scored against a fencer, and this is discouragingly no good. I also need my students to be able to reliably defend themselves and block more inbound attacks than get through and touch target.

One-and-done does not cut it in fencing. Getting my students to be consistent in the execution of the techniques is how they will become good, if not great, fencers. This is why we go over the mechanics of the motions. This is why I explain to them how the moves work. This is why we review the permutations of the available options, so my students can decide which variation they like best and when to use which option. Having choices may seem counter-intuitive to consistency, but it is not unless the person with the options does not understand how to pick which selection in what situation. Remember: reality itself is not always consistent.

In business, successful execution relies on consistency in software systems, business operations, data governance, supply chains, and people. First and foremost, if your business does not have consistency established with regards to procedures, software use, data integrity, supply chain partners, and personnel responsibilities, then your organization risks not being able to execute consistently to the satisfaction of the customer. Inconsistency breeds waste and waste translates to higher operating costs and equates to inefficiency.

Second, to be consistent a business should have a backup plan. A fencer in a competition has backup equipment at-the-ready because equipment can fail. Weapons can break, wires can snap, lames (the metallic jackets used in foil and sabre) can have bad spots. Competitive fencers have plenty of backup equipment that they can swap out so they can continue fencing their bout if a failure occurred. If a fencer in a competition could not replace equipment immediately, they would very likely be forced to forfeit the match, and this would be a heck of a way to lose.

A business needs to decide what mission-critical systems, partners, employees, machines it is reliant upon that are individual, sole-source, one-of-a-kind, or unique that the company would struggle to do without if suddenly removed or unavailable. These represent real threats to the organization, not in their singular existence, but in their potential lack of availability, that would render the business unable to be consistent in its operation and thus delivery of its product or service.

Lesson Learned

Fencers understand that consistency is more than just proper training to ensure the body and the mind are developed to be able to rapidly respond to the competitive challenge on the fencing strip. Consistency is also about ensuring that the fencer will have the necessary backup equipment should any of their primary equipment fail during a bout. And while I focused on competitive fencers, the need for backup equipment really does apply to all fencers: everyone in my club has at least some extra equipment (e.g. a spare weapon, extra weapon tips, multiple gloves) because equipment just wears out. Certainly, as the club owner and coach, I make sure I have sufficient extra everything.

Keeping consistency in business means ensuring data is backed up, software systems are able to be co-located or relocated and employees reconnected in a short timeframe if the building suffers from a disaster (e.g. hurricane, twister, earthquake, flood, fire), suppliers/vendors are continually monitored for risk, and procedures are documented so that employees out sick or on vacation can have their tasks handled in the interim without business operations coming to a halt. Business organizations need to examine their execution chain and understand what they lack in redundancy that could go wrong that could affect their ability to satisfy their customer commitments. With this understanding, what is the backup plan for if, or when, a critical component becomes unreliable? Does your business understand which customers would – and would not – be sympathetic to failures to fulfill orders? How long can your business survive without the ability to provide its goods or services? More about the importance of backups in fencing and in business shortly.

Lesson Twenty-Two: Using Visual Indicators

In fencing, the relative distance between the tips of the weapons are a visual indicator to the fencers as to whether or not they are within successful striking distance to their opponents. The general rule of thumb is that if the tip of your weapon is approximately 25% of the way down from the top of the opponent's blade from a relative distance (meaning that your weapon does not have to be in direct contact with your opponent's blade), you are very likely within striking distance to your opponent. Conversely, of course, if the tip of your opponent's blade is at approximately 25% down relative distance from the tip of your blade, and you are just standing there and not thinking about defending yourself, you will likely have a point scored against you in the very near future unless your opponent is just as frozen in the moment as you are. An opponent who is positioning their weapon at such proximity to yours is likely maneuvering to attack.

Because fencers also calibrate each other, a fencer looks at the opponent for tell-tale signs of an action, such as a visual indicator that the opponent may be launching an attack. Some fencers like to create distance before their attacks by backing up a few steps and taking a run at their opponents; as such, the pattern of moving backward several steps would be a good visual indicator that the challenging fencer was about to attack. Other fencers may crouch down more before they execute a lunge in order to gain more spring in their action.

In business, visual indicators can be manual or electronic and are used to signal a person into action, in order words, to attack a problem. Examples of where visual indicators are used include: supply chain, manufacturing, inventory, and accounting. A visual indicator in business can be an email alert, a light that either flashes or suddenly turns on or changes in color, a text message, a graphical dashboard signal, or an exception report. Visual alerts in business rely on the underlying data being accurate, containing or excluding the proper set of data, and correctly setting the alert signal trigger.

The fencer who fails to see an opponent's visual signals will be remiss in understanding when an opponent is likely to be on the attack or to be able to take advantage of flaws in an opponent's defenses. Without the ability to properly calibrate one's opponent by understanding their visual signals, a fencer is likely subject to being more on the defensive rather than to be able to be the successful attacker.

Organizations that fail to establish visual alerts of problems or do not adjust their alert signals as the business changes, run the real risk of not being informed of critical conditions that can negatively impact execution and disable the ability to provide quality and timely goods and services to customers. High accounts receivables balances, supplier risk profiles, customer backorders, inventory shortages (whether for raw materials or finished goods), and equipment or machine maintenance signals are just some of the key visual indicators that organizations should be continually aware of.

Lesson Learned

Visual indicators play a very important role in fencing: they provide the ability for a fencer to pierce more deeply into the mindset of their opponent and allow the fencer to judge, if not anticipate, the actions of the competition more effectively.

In business, the failure to establish and use visual alerts can cause the organization to miss critical operational execution failures that impact customer satisfaction. While not all alerts can proactively prevent an execution failure, alerts can help to warn of impending, immediate, or recent problems to which the organization can begin a communication campaign, take another form of corrective action like data analysis, or initiate preventative maintenance. Without such alerts, the organization would never know that a problem existed at all until much too late, and perhaps until the problem manifested into something worse.

Over-stimulation from too many alerts is a common business condition. I have seen situations where excessive – and unnecessary – messages have clogged email systems and reports to the point of burying important signals. This mixture makes it very difficult to discern the superfluous from the serious such that the message recipients are frustrated whereby they just overlook the report entirely. In business, visual indicators should typically alert to an exception. Warnings are okay to include, and some systems that create green-yellow-red alert indicators have the benefit of advising of pending problems. Visual indicators are functionally important but their overuse in business can create a situation of distraction and disregard rather than proper functional use.

Visual indicators should take into consideration individuals who may have difficulties discerning colors, in which case fill patterns should be incorporated as well as colors when producing dashboard and spreadsheet graphics.

Referring back to a fencer's use of touch and sound, indicators need not always be visual. Industrial barcode scanners used in noisy warehouse environments are designed to vibrate in different patterns to advise the user of good versus bad scan reads, e.g. vibrate on a good scan and not vibrate on a bad scan, or to vibrate differently whether the scan read was successful or not.

Lesson Twenty-Three: Have a Backup... And Another Backup

In fencing competitions, fencers really rely solely on their own equipment. Weapons can break, wires in body cords will go bad, connections can become faulty. Backup equipment, and backup equipment to the backup equipment, must be at-the-ready to swap or else the fencer will in all likelihood have to yield the bout to the opponent due to an equipment malfunction, and that is no way to have to lose a competition. If I am going down, I am going down fighting and against a better opponent. To have to withdraw from a bout just because I did not have a spare mask, weapon, lame, glove, or body cord is wholly unacceptable.

As such, to not have a backup for each spare is just not worth the risk. The return on the investment is well justified: either the fencer ensures a sequence of working equipment is at the ready or the fencer is forced to withdraw from a bout. Given the relatively moderate prices of the equipment costs, it is simply not worth the price of a spare item or two versus the risk of primary and even secondary item failure and subsequent bout withdrawal (and thus resultant loss) due to not having proper, functional backup equipment ready and waiting.

But businesses make this mistake all of the time. Businesses rely on a single printer, piece of manufacturing equipment, supplier/vendor, employee, or data backup (if a data backup exists at all!) without any thought given to the 'what if' disaster scenario.

In business, especially for software systems, backups are an absolute must. Most companies are at the point where backups are performed and stored off-site nowadays. Just because software is moving to the cloud does not mean that the data does not have to be backed up. Having a 'cloud' system can be one of several different technology models. So, if you have software running in 'the cloud' what is your cloud software system model and what does your data backup and retention policy look like?

Is it your servers on-site hosting your software? Is it your servers off-site hosting your software? Is it your software hosted on someone else's servers? Is it someone else's software hosted on theirs or someone else's servers? 'The cloud,' as basically defined, is simply networked computers accessible through the Internet. So, who owns it and where it is located are not just trivial matters anymore, because there is considerable risk and responsibility for upkeep, uptime, protection from harmful viruses and malicious attacks, and security of sensitive data. One service company I was helping became embroiled in a significant problem when their cloud software company refused to continue providing services, and withheld access to their data over a contract dispute. This effectively shut down the service company's business lock, stock, and barrel for over one solid week, and left the service company limping along for several weeks – with the ramifications extending into the following months – thereafter. Had the service company performed proper data backups from the cloud software provider like I continually recommended, the service company could have avoided much of this disaster and moved rapidly to a new solution company.

What about the business procedures that employees are performing? Does anyone really know or understand the daily processes that are being performed to operate the business? Are people's tasks documented? Are other people assigned as backup personnel to the primary task doers, and are these backup people familiar with the current state of the operations tasks and software systems? When was the last time the backup was asked to perform the primary person's role? Employees do tend to take sick days, vacation time, and will leave companies with little more than two weeks' notice.

Supply chain risk identification looks at suppliers/vendors who are sole-source or majority-source providers of mission-critical goods and services. This includes raw materials inventory suppliers/vendors and service providers such as contract manufacturers and third-party logistics companies for warehousing, distribution, and shipping services. If your organization is wholly or majorly dependent upon an outside company for goods or services, this external company should be monitored for its health and stability on a very regular basis. Even large and very large companies have been known to fail, so your business should have in-place a supplier/vendor monitoring program. Even if you do not decide to divide your business across multiple suppliers/vendors for a particular product or service to reduce risk, ensuring that you discuss the state of health with your current critical suppliers/vendors on a regular basis will go a long way to ensuring you avoid potential stoppage or shutdown disaster.

Lesson Learned

The old adage about being penny wise and pound foolish is very applicable to the discussion of having the right backups, and note I used the plural 'backups' and not the singular 'backup.' In fencing, whether for leisure or competition, equipment failure is a guarantee that we accept and prepare for. Yes, there is a cost for the extra equipment but it is a worthwhile investment versus the risk of not being able to participate in fencing, or worse, to not be able to continue in a competition.

In business, there needs to be an examination of the internal and external risks which require the organization to consider the appropriate level of replication. Software systems need to have their software and data backed up, but as tradition would have it, do not store the backup in the office itself because if something happens to the office (e.g. fire, flood, earthquake) all is absolutely lost. The business should examine its processes and ensure they are documented so the loss – either temporary (e.g. illness, vacation) or permanent of a key employee (which most staffers seem to be these days) will not cause major operational chaos.

The organization should examine its internal and external supply chain, reviewing mission-critical suppliers/vendors and machines/equipment. If backups to providers are needed and some aspects of the business are best divided among multiple suppliers/vendors, then that decision should be considered. If machines or equipment is aging and spare parts are becoming problematic, stocking some extras as they become available would be a wise decision if fully replacing the machine or equipment is not a current option.

Lesson Twenty-Four: Leaders Need to Think Like Fencers

Part of teaching a sport like fencing is that I have to teach my students to think like fencers. To simply have my students repeat the attacks, parries, and ripostes robotically is missing a critical comprehension component of what it is to be a fencer. I expect my students to be – to become – fencers within the fabric of their being. They have to embody the spirit of what it is to hold a sword in their hand and know how to wield it well. They have to understand what it is to think like a fencer.

Thinking like a fencer involves believing in one's abilities. Confidence without cockiness is how a fellow consultant who was a former chief information officer at an industry-leading consumer products retailer once described me to a rather arrogant, obstinate, and belligerent self-titled director of information technology during a consulting assignment. Poise and grace in a fencer are requirements: the ability to maintain one's balance and assuredness in the face of an aggressive opponent is what helps tilt the scale in a fencer's favor. Just like a talented fencer uses their opponent's strengths against them, a fencer's over-aggressive behavior can be used against them too. It is typically counter-productive and can very well be a contributing factor to a fencer's downfall in a bout.

(I was asked by a vice president at the company I was helping to mentor this aforementioned director of information technology into his role. I was happy to do so and approached the information technology director with my assignment. He admitted that his lack of confidence in his role was the cause of his confrontational battles and attitude problems. I told him that I would help him through his personal and professional challenges that were affecting his on-the-job performance. Regrettably, he only self-destructed, sabotaging himself, and eventually, the company removed him from employment permanently.)

A fencer's confidence extends to the belief in the attack: that it is the right thing to do at the right time. That the attack maneuver selected is the proper strategy to execute and, perhaps most importantly, that the attack will succeed and the target will be touched for a successful score. As such, the fencer executes the attack with 100% of all resources (e.g. speed, strength, force) without fear of the attack failing. The fencer knows that should the attack not succeed, the fencer has the wherewithal and the resources the mount what is expected to be a successful defense, and will then return to attack again at the proper time. After all, despite the confidence that all will go according to the primary plan, having a backup plan is simply a smart idea.

Business leaders plot their organization's go-forward strategies and decide what projects to pursue and what projects to put on hold. In selecting the go-forward projects, business leaders must showcase the confidence they have in their teams in conceiving of the projects and in their organizations for the execution of the projects. Leadership decides that each project contributes to the organization's overall objective and that each individual project will be executed strategically the right way as to best benefit the business. When is it the right time to attack, and when is it prudent to sit tight and patiently wait, e.g. for the market to decide on a standard?

Leaders cannot pick a project that they suspect will fail, or select a project that they are not completely confident is a good project for the company, e.g. one that the company is not resourced adequately to successfully accomplish. This lack of confidence is not healthy for the organization. Nor should leadership oversell a project too early in its lifecycle. Yes, there needs to be some cheerleading about what the results of a project will accomplish for the business. However, similar to a fencer's attack, the business should never count the score until the touchpoint is made. Just like a fencer's attack which can be withdrawn during the course of the attack if the fencer believes it is strategically beneficial to do so, business projects can get halted or misdirected, albeit for more complex and costly reasons. But it is far better to cancel a bad project early – or as soon as the realization is determined – than to let it get too far down the road and manifest itself into something costlier and more disruptive – or destructive – to the organization. Certain projects with high visibility that are oversold that shake the confidence of customers and employees are damaging to the images of these businesses in the eyes of those internal and external stakeholders.

Like the participant who learns to think like a fencer, business executives need to learn to think like the leaders that they are. The projects that they promote cannot be for personal reward or gain, they cannot be for political or prideful purposes, nor can they be ill-conceived for reasons less than otherwise legitimate, e.g. to whitewash the value of the company for an upcoming set of prospective buyers. Not all attacks succeed, but as long as they are planned with a purpose and executed with the confidence that they will result in a scoring touch, at least the attack was performed in earnest. And if it doesn't work either during or at the end, in any case a skilled fencer can recover and return to attack again. And for the business, if it comes to that conclusion, I hope it is realized much earlier rather than too late.

Lesson Learned

A significant part of coaching fencing is teaching my students the mindset of a fencer. This mindset involves achieving confidence in one's skills; the ability to make a decision and then committing to that choice; the knowledge that changing one's mind is okay. But I tell my students that what is not okay is not committing 100% to the execution of that entire plan: that not having the confidence in the success of the plan (e.g. the attack) is something that they have to push out of their minds.

This is not a contradiction. What I am simply stating is that, upon careful consideration, if you are going to attack, do so fully. As you have learned, part of the attack's decision tree is that the attack can be altered or stopped, but if you are going to start one, start it full-on.

Not every attack will succeed, and that is not just a good fencing lesson, it is a good life lesson. (Yes, the conversations at my fencing club sometimes go far and beyond just fencing.) If your attack fails, have the confidence in your parry to defend yourself and recover to attack again. But never – ever – not commit completely to an attack because of the fear of failure. That is not acceptable. Typically, over-confidence is not a problem, but when it is, I calm the student down and focus them on the basics, reminding them to go through the process steps I have taught them. It is when the student goes through the process first that they create a doable attack plan that has a better chance of success.

Successful business leaders and fencers do think alike in the reality that effective business leaders must exhibit the same attack-type confidence in order to push their organizations forward. And that patiently going through the process helps to ensure that the plan succeeds. What the strategic thinking fencer does in seconds is expanded into days, weeks, and months for business leaders who need proper time to analyze and plan strategic projects and the underlying tasks, but the comparison remains true. Thoughtful business leaders must ensure their plan (attack) is the right strategy at the right time and must go forward with confidence, always ready and accepting that change in direction may and is likely to be required. Proper planning should reduce the need to fully halt the attack (cancel the project), and this goes hand-in-hand with balancing confidence and cockiness. One way to accomplish this is by going back and re-reading the chapter in this book on calibrating one's opponent and self-assessment. Sometimes, too many times, businesses are their own worst enemy, and this comes from the inability to fully understand themselves as an organization, which is a leadership failure, a trap I ensure my student fencers do not get caught in.

Lesson Twenty-Five: Fencing Is Physical Chess... So Is Business

While ballet is apparently the dance form of fencing, fencing is unquestionably the physical form of chess. The sport of fencing is actually known by its nickname as 'physical chess.' A fencer is taught to think two moves ahead. For example, if the fencer attacks, what are the possible parry moves the opponent can execute, and for each parry option, what are the counter attacks (ripostes) available to the defending fencer? These permutations are not necessarily fixed (inasmuch as they are of a limited number) as they can be dependent upon each fencer's unique style. Nor, of course, are they set in stone as a fencer can feint in one path only to suddenly change using, for example, a coupé or disengage, and opt for a new track to a now open target area of the opponent. So, what move actually happens when are typically random. When I instruct my students, we go through the various possibilities available so my students can understand that doing what the opponent does not expect is one of the keys to success in fencing. Therefore, varying the attacks, parries, and ripostes is critically important in keeping an opponent off guard and achieving touchpoints. To become transparent to the opponent by selecting and executing the same attack and defense moves all of the time allows the opponent to easily calibrate the fencer, anticipate the fencer's moves, and succeed in defeating their cookie-cutter challenger.

As previously discussed, as a fencing coach I don't just teach how to execute the moves, I also teach the mindset of fencing. As part of thinking like a fencer, I push my students to think two moves ahead, to learn to anticipate, to see the various possibilities, to select an option out of a series of choices. And in fencing, to do all of this within sometimes not more than a second or so due to the speed of the sport.

In business, the ability – no, the necessity – to examine all possibilities and understand their consequences is of preeminent importance as a critical thinking skill. Businesses create strategic plans that must be broken down into tactical moves in order to be executed. Are those the right strategies for the organization? What are the short-term and long-term impacts of those plans on the business? How will the interim execution of the tactics toward the completion of the strategies impact the organization? Will the business become less of a competitor for a while? Will the business have to delay introducing new items or updated products or additional services for a certain time period? How will this affect revenue, the ability to satisfy current customer demands, and the ability to acquire new customers?

Business leaders as creative strategists may not be the best tacticians when it comes to an examination and execution of the details of the plans. A fencer is both the creative strategist and the tactical doer just like a chess player who devises the move and physically moves the piece on the board. But in business, with its organizational hierarchical layers and greater complexity, the same person or persons creating the strategy, e.g. 'We need new business software,' may not be the same people who will accomplish the ground-level tactical details of gathering the requirements, vetting the software vendors, converting and migrating the data, matching the operational tasks to the software functionality, and doing the training.

Businesses fail when they do not consider the consequences of their actions due to myopic outlook. But this cannot simply be constrained to the short-term cause-and-effect of immediate decisions: organizations can, and will, suffer irreparable harm due to a lack of forethought when there is a failure to think beyond the present. Wrapping together several concepts already discussed in this book: both a fencer and a business leader must have the confidence in their decision of an attack plan and execute it to the fullest extent of their resources, including defensive abilities. They must have the ability to foresee and understand the potential consequences, thinking two (or more) steps ahead, avoiding or maneuvering around obstacles in the way whenever possible. Should the attack require a sudden alteration, a change can be inserted into the plan as an option. If the attack needs to be halted for good reason then so be it, better to bail on an attack early before full failure than later when it is likely to prove to be costlier.

But if there was better forethought, would not the right attack have been initially planned in the first place? Inasmuch as there are uncontrollable variables in both fencing and business – in fencing, the opponent is not controllable, in business, there are many competitive considerations, market forces and internal issues that are not controllable – that would cause a change to an attack, certainly, an initial selection of the right attack minimizes a need for alterations during the attack itself. Part of the selection of the correct attack comes from the result of calibration, of the opponent and of oneself be it the fencer or the business.

Readers might wonder if the ability to think two moves ahead may cause what is known as 'paralysis by analysis' to occur. This is the symptom (as previously mentioned) where nothing is done because a person is continually over-thinking a problem and cannot decide on possible outcome or determine a suitable resolution. After all, a fencer has to work through the set of possibilities in a fractional amount of time. This is where some of the mindset training comes in that I teach: decide what you want to do and do it. But I don't teach my students to select their attacks or parries willy-nilly without purposeful thought. I am trained in the skill of faster decision making. Ascertain the black-and-white facts as presented within the context, process them, and determine what is the best course of action. It is how I think. While I cannot speak for all of my students, it is how I attempt to coach them in their fencing mindset too. And like anything else, especially in fencing, it doesn't necessarily come easy and as such, it takes a lot of practice and is likely dependent upon the individual person.

Lesson Learned

Success is more readily achieved when obstacles are anticipated. These obstacles, risks to the success of reaching the goal, are ideally to be avoided or mitigated. (In fencing, avoidance of the opponent's weapon on the attack is optimal but sometimes unavoidable.) But if these obstacles are completely unknown then they are more of a danger, as they are not visible and thus their impact on the success of reaching target cannot be predicted with any certainty. It is this uncertainty that causes project plans to go so awry when obstacles are thrown in the path. At least in fencing, we know what the primary obstacle is: the opponent's weapon.

It is the fencer's ability to think two moves ahead that helps the fencer avoid, or mitigate, failure in the first place. The ability to calibrate the opponent helps the fencer determine the best strategic move to execute. Should anything go wrong, the experienced fencer automatically knows how to recover and return to the fight. Yes, points will be scored for and against, but it is the nature of the sport. Not every business project succeeds on the exact time and budget, but as long as they are as close as possible, given the myriad of variables and uncontrollable factors that come in to play are considered and handled, the projects are generally scored as successes as long as the output meets the customer requirements.

Business leaders – in their rush to success – may too often focus on the results and not the process, or the goal and not the hazardous journey to get there. Strategic thinking and tactical analysis can help leaders understand the pros and cons of certain decisions, assist in avoiding costly mistakes, and provide a futuristic-type perspective on the ramifications of their decisions on the organization. Thinking two moves ahead aids in avoiding executional pitfalls by envisioning what could lie henceforth and minimizing the need to recover from what was unexpected.

Lesson Twenty-Six: Small Steps Lead to Big Successes

Many new students who come into my fencing club do so having already watched fencing videos on the Internet, usually selecting Olympic-level competitions to view. They are impressed by the combination of fierceness and composure the sport requires.

Inasmuch as the weapon work is what students really gravitate to, the mastery of the footwork is a critical component of being a successful fencer. In establishing the footwork, a fencer first decides whether they will fence right-handed or left-handed. Then, the matching leg of the weapon arm is advanced forward a bit with the front foot pointed forward toward the opponent. The foot of the rear leg is turned outward away from the body. With the heels of the feet aligned, the feet are perpendicular to each other. (This positioning causes the torso – the largest single target area on a fencer – to angle with reference to the opponent.) The distance between the feet is enough to where the fencer can be in a crouch position with the knees bent and be comfortable: the distance between the feet is not too close and not too far apart as to allow for good balance and movement. Shoulders should be parallel to the floor.

Footwork in fencing allows the fencer to control their speed, distance, direction, balance, and the tempo (which I consider to be a different concept than the overall speed) of the competition. Sometimes, I need to simply rely on my ability to be faster than my opponent. At other times, I need to change the rhythm (tempo) of what is happening: to either speed up or slow down the action in contrast to what I believe my opponent is comfortable with or anticipating. I use distance both offensively and defensively, sometimes changing direction suddenly, and I use my footwork to control this capability and the proximity to my opponent. And without a doubt, my footwork is the foundation of my balance and poise. Weapon work alone does not win the battle; my footwork mastery is just as important as my skill with a sword.

Footwork in fencing is based on relatively small steps performed in a rapid-fire sequence; the movements are not large gallops or leaps. The more that your feet are in contact with the floor, the more control you have; conversely, of course, the less time your feet are in contact with the floor, the less control you have. In my calibration of my opponent, if I see an opponent leaping or galloping, I will seek to take advantage of that lack of control by my opponent and likely attack when my opponent has no control of their footwork, e.g. when my opponent is airborne. Footwork control enables the ability to be agile, to change direction quickly, to alter tempo and direction instantly, to increase or decrease speed on demand. Footwork control enables the fencer to better react to the continually changing competitive situation of the challenge.

Businesses have big projects such as software system implementations and process improvement missions. But these big projects cannot be successful by taking big leaps and gallops at the tasks that need to be done. Successful projects are separated into tasks which are then further divided into smaller steps. In today's modern software development climate, projects are performed under an 'agile' methodology which seeks to propel development more quickly by reducing the scope of the individual requirement to something small and manageable. When I began my programming (known today as 'software development') career, we employed a relatively new methodology called 'top-down' which was a similar divide-and-conquer approach. Terms and names may change, but winning philosophies remain the same. Start with the big ideas and whittle them down to smaller, manageable tasks that can be easily programmed, even to the point where the code or concept can be reusable. Business operations process definition follows in the same footsteps, with the pun absolutely intended here: starting with the big picture, define-and-sequence the tasks into smaller, manageable, ordered, and repeatable steps.

Lesson Learned

Names may change but the timeless concepts remain sound and secure. Smaller steps, when executed in rapid succession – assuming that the entity (person, business) is proficient enough to do so – enable better progression by successfully accomplishing smaller goals in greater number more quickly. This boosts performance by overcoming the psychological barrier to success versus failing to achieve when trying to succeed against a big obstacle. New fencers are able to get their footwork skills sharpened more quickly by getting more steps correct as soon as possible versus fewer steps correct over an extended period of time. Similarly, project successes come from accomplishing smaller tasks in rapid succession and building upon the accomplishments of the previous steps. It is easier to learn from these smaller more frequent successes than from occasional successes or failures.

But true to form, things don't always go as planned. Stuff happens. Changes in direction and speed are to be expected both in fencing and in business. Taking smaller, more measured steps allows for risks to be better managed, changes to have a lesser impact on the overall plan, and for recovery to have a better chance of occurring.

Inasmuch as we may all want to make the great, single leap toward triumph, it only happens in rare occurrences such as buying that once-in-a-lifetime lottery ticket. Otherwise, smaller steps – when executed with professionalism and precision – offer the best opportunity to quickly move toward big achievements while successfully allowing navigational changes when necessary. And if I have to make a sudden stop, I would rather have to halt after being fully in control from making smaller, faster steps than needing to do so after taking a large, reckless leap.

Lesson Twenty-Seven: Some Battle Costs Are Not Worth the Price

I have already stated that I teach my fencing students all that I know, including my little tips and tricks that I use in my style of fencing. But I think I need to qualify when I say that I teach my students 'tricks.' There is nothing unscrupulous or unethical or illegal about what I teach my students to do that I do myself. I have standard maneuvers that I execute very well that surprise my students because I make them look so easy. Other advanced moves are a little bit complicated, especially for beginners, so I don't use them on new students. After all, my purpose is to teach, not to overwhelm or to prove I am some kind of champion. There is no honor in beating a youngster or an inexperienced opponent, and I don't go around bragging about either or any such sort of victory.

Some fencers will let out a yell when they attack. I don't do this, though I sometimes will let out an exertional grunt, not unlike a tennis player who is contacting the tennis ball. The difference between the fencing yell and the exertional grunt is that in reality, the primary purpose of the fencing yell for some fencers is to distract the bout director's attention in order to have the attacking fencer's forward motion considered to be a valid right-of-way attack.

Despite the fact that competitive fencers are electronically wired to a scoring machine and there is at least one director watching, the issue of who commenced the attack can sometimes be vague given the speed at which fencing transpires. As such, yelling during the bout is designed to distract the director for the purpose of making the director believe that the fencer yelling the loudest had the right of the attack. Remember that foil and sabre are right-of-way weapons, which means that the only the fencer with the right of the attack – the fencer who initiated and continued the first aggressive motion – has the permission to score at that moment. Two fencers who appear to attack simultaneously may only have their attack timing separated by a fraction of a second in reality.

I don't teach my fencing students to yell or scream or otherwise distract the director; I don't believe in the need for having to do so. I don't teach my fencing students to do anything but fence to their best confidence and abilities using the skills they inherently have. If they need to use some chicanery to win, they need to fence somewhere else other than my club. I do not tolerate cheating or deceit to justify winning.

In business, as part of the culture of the organization, is there an attitude of winning at all costs? If so, there is a price to be paid for that cultural degradation because it will infect the company, the employees, the suppliers/vendors, and the customers. The price of winning at all costs will result in an alienation between the organization and its key stakeholders (employees, customers, suppliers/vendors) because the organization will drive a wedge between itself and its stakeholders as it looks out only for itself and not its invested, critical partners.

The price to be paid for winning at all costs is the capitulation of ethics, values, and morals in lieu revenue, or what I should qualify as what is certain to be 'short term' revenue. Companies cannot survive high employee turnover and the disruptive loss of knowledge and experience. The cost to acquire a new customer is five to ten times the cost of existing customer retention. A loyal supplier/vendor can be a business-saving partner in a time of crisis, and an invaluable cost-saving collaborator during times of change and disruption.

Short-term gains under unprincipled decision-making will have long-term negative impacts. This goes beyond not performing the due diligence necessary prior to decision-making: this is the egregious disregard for what is right over the embracement of what is wrong for reasons that are absolutely unacceptable.

Lesson Learned

An organization's culture includes establishing the figurative compass, determining whether the directional arrow will be allowed to point true and if the organization will be permitted to follow the proper path. This decision starts with the senior leaders and trickles down through the middle managers and continues with the staff employees. (Reflect back to the COSO framework aspect of the Control

Environment, also known as the 'Tone at the Top.') The cultural vibe will be felt beyond the organization to all of the stakeholders: employees, customers, suppliers/vendors alike.

The corporate world has at times regrettably perverted the perspective of what it means to be competitive. You can still a ruthless challenger yet do so wholly ethically. How? By being smarter, nimbler, and more creative than your competitor. By using all of your strengths to their fullest extent. By calibrating your opponents and finding and exploiting their weaknesses in a competitive but not corrupt way. But surrendering yourself and your soul for the sake of a win? Cheating for a championship? That is a price to be paid, and those are prizes that are just not worth the cost.

Behavior, whether bad or good, is learned and mimicked. It can also be repeated and reverberated back out of necessity. Business that wonder why employees act the way they do, why customers are leaving, why suppliers/vendors no longer provide priority, likely only need to look themselves in the mirror to determine whether a strategy of winning at all costs in the short-term was a smart long-term plan.

Lesson Twenty-Eight: Don't Overlook Opportunities

Fencers are not handed gold-engraved invitations that inform or invite them to attack their targets. A fencer – in calibrating their opponent and observing visual indicators that represent possible openings or advantages – look for the right opportunity to strike at the right time. Are the opponent's feet too close together or too far apart, rendering the opponent less mobile or momentarily immobile? Did the opponent lower or shift their weapon, leaving an avenue of attack available to an open area of target?

A fencer has very little time to decide whether to attack or not. As the saying goes, sometimes you have to strike while the proverbial iron is hot. I will add that sometimes you also have to strike when you just think that the iron is hot, or going to be hot, meaning that you won't always know if the opportunity outcome is favorable or not, but sometimes you just have to go for it based on the assessment of all accumulated knowledge you have at the moment. As I have discussed, a fencer who is confident in their skills will attack with 100% force upon deciding that attacking is the correct decision. If the attack fails (or has to be withdrawn), the fencer will rely on their confident defenses to guard against the opponent's counter-strike. Does this always work to the fencer's advantage? No, but in the attack-parry-riposte scenario, a fencer cannot let the occasional missed or failed opportunity get them down. To lose the mental aspect is certainly to lose the entire bout. Planned, thoughtfully-considered attacks that don't touch target are nothing to be embarrassed about; it is the ill-conceived attacks that a fencer should reconsider as to whether they were the right thing to do at the right time.

Opportunities to strike – in fencing, in business – don't come along as often as we would sometimes like or at the times we would prefer, so we have to be ready (en garde, a.k.a. on guard) to take advantage of them when we can. But not as many businesses do this as they should, and this executional failure results in fewer wins and more losses which creates additional challenges for the organization. Worse, there are actually more misses than hits because the overlooked opportunities will not be obvious to the untrained eye.

A reason that businesses fail to avail themselves of opportunities is because they are focusing on the wrong target, something I have mentioned previously and one of the themes of this book. Some organizations are so focused on meeting a made-up end-of-month number, sticking to a fictitious budgetary figure, or holding fast to a concocted margin percentage, that they forgo opportunities to promote themselves and gain visibility, reduce project risk, or satisfy their customer demands.

Don't get me wrong: as a business professional who helps companies boost performance via analyzing data and improve operating efficiencies, setting metrics and examining key performance indicators, I am in complete agreement that it is important for organizations to analyze their activities. But companies that pervert this analysis by, for example, constantly prioritizing the size of the win over the win itself are, in my opinion, probably lacking in some creative and critical thinking perspective. A return-on-investment analysis has to consider the rather intangible yet impactful cost of what happens should the opportunity presented be taken versus passed-over. It is not always a matter of dollars and cents, but sometimes more so an issue of dollars and (common) sense.

Companies that have the ability to educate their employees for reasonable costs, but don't. Businesses avoid sending employee representatives to conferences because it was 'not in the budget' even though it is the right place to be, but the notification was not presented at the right time (when the budget was being prepared). Organizations lose money to customer penalties due to supply chain execution issues but instead of getting qualified help to fix the root cause issues, they just continue to suffer performance problems and financial losses.

Lesson Learned

In fencing, a fencer must be able to identify opportunities to attack by calibrating the opponent. The fencer can also create opportunities to attack through feint maneuvers that cause the opponent's weapon to shift position or over-compensate and leave a new avenue for attack available. Overcoming the fear of failure – having the confidence in themselves – enables the fencer to attack the opponent with all of the fencer's might once the opportunity to attack is presented.

In business, opportunities to advance the business include employee education, visibility promotions, conference attendance, consultant advice, quality improvements, software investment, and product or service development. All of these opportunities should be means toward an end result: growth of the company or executional improvement that better enables fulfillment of customer orders/service and enhances customer satisfaction. Opportunities do not always present themselves at the most convenient of times, and they will certainly require an expenditure of time and or money, though typically both. Companies that continue to consider their cash as sacrosanct over their ultimate success need to understand that opportunities to attack problems and strike at one's challenges and challengers don't always come along when they want, so they have to take advantage of them when they do. And sometimes opportunities to strike have to be created by ourselves. Organizations can be aggressive attackers or passive defenders in how they approach opportunities to advance their agendas. It is only the attacker, and not the defender, who has the potential to score a touchpoint, but only when an attack is launched, and done so at the opportune time.

Lesson Twenty-Nine:
Are You Adaptable?

Learning to switch from being a right-handed to left-handed fencer to allow my right shoulder to recover from the injury I incurred while playing racquetball was a tough transition to make. It was, nevertheless, a necessary decision if I was going to continue to be involved in a sport that gave me real enjoyment as a participant and an instructor. It was a tough three-month transition, but I started out with a belief that I could be successful, and as is so often true, that is really a first and foremost factor in being able to accomplish something. Thankfully, I am a creative person and have a good amount of spontaneity mixed in, so I often just figure out how to get things accomplished that need to get done. This certainly is a help to me personally, but it is a real proven benefit professionally much to the delight of the companies I help especially when it comes to meeting project timelines and budgets while creatively solving operations, software, and data challenges, often with just the tools I have at the time.

When I change up and switch from right-to-left hand on my students, they usually complain that it's difficult because fencing an opposite-handed (notably left-handed) opponent is typically more of a challenge, which it basically is. But my students do not initially realize the one-two benefit that they have with an ambidextrous coach: my dual-handed capability better prepares them for the real-world of competitive fencing where they will most certainly duel against a left-handed fencer at some point. And because I know that my students will inevitably face an opposite-handed opponent – even my left-handed students may struggle against a left-handed opponent because they have only practiced against right-handed fencers – I need to ensure that my students are adaptable to whatever situations they may encounter when they leave my club. I am admittedly a little nurturing in that way.

From a business perspective, adaption to change is crucial for an organization to be successful. I have proposed many business concepts in this book which I know first-hand are successful when embraced and properly implemented. An organization first has to accept the fact that it must change to survive, just like I had to realize that I had to learn to adapt to a new form of fencing to be able to continue.

When other coaches or instructors come into my club to fence, they instinctively want to help as it is their instructional nature to do so. Somewhat sheepishly, they ask if it is okay if they get involved in training my participants, as they may see a fencer waiting during a break or see a fencer in need of corrective action. No one has ever come into my club to try and take over, imposing their teaching style to supplant my own methods, nor do I take offense at their offers of assistance. These other coaches or instructors are simply offering their suggestions as nothing more than their being kind enough to go beyond just being there for enjoyment and having a willingness to help. I think all coaches know that individual instructors each have our own teaching methods but, a smart educator will understand that we can always learn new educational tips and tricks from other instructors and should always take the opportunity to avail ourselves when it is presented to us.

Businesses, in adapting, first need to come to the realization that they need to change in order to continue progressing successfully. This can be a big awareness revelation that takes a long time coming, and probably the most significant step to make in the overall process. Next, there is the belief that the organization can actually change and successfully do at least some things it does differently. This speaks to company culture, including leadership. Does the company have the inherent confidence in itself that it can change to overcome the obstacles against it and meet the new challenges it is confronting? There will be struggles in this journey, so the organization must determine if it has the willingness to undertake the difficulties it will face, the disappointments it is bound to encounter, in reaching its goals. Proper project management will divide-and-conquer the lofty goals into lower and more attainable tasks to keep the project humming along. Nonetheless, larger goals like software system go-live dates are bigtime project targets which are discouraging, and costly, to miss.

Is the organization willing to be coached into being a better performer? If my fencing students already knew how to fence well, they would not need to learn from a more experienced fencer like myself. I coach a variety of new and experienced participants: fencers home from their university sessions on break who want to continue and improve on their training; world-class fencers who seek alternate instruction perspectives; new fencers just starting out; fencers with experience who want to continue to enjoy the sport and get back into competing; fencers who just want to enjoy the sport and get some exercise.

Businesses sometimes – oftentimes – need outside assistance, instruction on how to do the things they do better, to try new things out, to see things differently, to adapt to changes more effectively, to fix problems causing executional failures. The investment in this help is returned many times over in the value – e.g. improvement savings, new opportunities, new directions – as they continue to benefit the organization. Just as athletes need coaching to perform better, so do businesses need coaching to execute their functions better.

Fencers need to be highly adaptable to change given the characteristic speed of the sport. This is just one of the multiple attributes of fencing that I embrace in my professional business career, along with the other lessons that I have outlined in this book, which I hope you have found enlightening and beneficial. But none of the lessons in this book will be of use unless your organization first and foremost understands that it must be willing to embrace the changes necessary to improve. Your company has to be willing to get help when it needs it and to accept the recommendations when they are provided.

Lesson Learned

If business is a sport, the company participants – its employees – are like the athletes. I submit again that there is no better comparison than that to fencing. If you are not attacking, you are defending. You need to calibrate your opponents, whether they be your competitors or market forces. A self-assessment is also a requirement to understand how your company compares against its competition. Distance adds a new perspective, you may be too close to see clearly. Focusing on the target and avoiding the obstacles in the way helps to ensure you'll score when you strike. A company needs to begin by building upon its basics – including its people, culture, software systems, and operational processes – before it can proclaim itself an experienced champion. So regardless of it all, if you aren't a healthy athlete, and accept that you might have to make some changes to become one, you won't be able to sustain as a participant for very long.

Lesson Thirty: All for One and One for All

Many of you will recognize the title of this lesson: It is the beginning of the famous line from Alexandre Dumas's classic novel 'The Three Musketeers', that goes in full: 'All for one and one for all; united we stand, divided we fall.' The meaning is two-fold: 'All for one' means that the group or community supports each of the individual members, leaving no person behind should the team falter. 'One for all' means that each person contributes their own independent and unique strengths and skills to the collective group, supporting the team if there is trouble. The second part of the phrase captures the consequences of what will happen if the team does or does not adhere to the first part of the phrase: together the team will be successful ('united we stand'); apart, the group will falter and fail ('divided we fall'). I cannot think of a better comparison to represent the ideal corporate culture and environment which companies should strive to create than that of the Musketeers' creed.

A New York Times article published in September 26, 2018, Miami Herald newspaper reported on a study whose results were released the previous week in the Mayo Clinic

Proceedings. This was a follow-up study to research done in 2017 which analyzed 80,000 British men and women and discovered that those who played racquet sports tended to outlive those who were joggers. The new study returned to the same data source: the Copenhagen City Heart Study which continuously tracks the health of thousands of men and women in the study's named city and their participation in one of eight common sports in Denmark, including: cycling, swimming, tennis, soccer, and badminton. The research then focused on 8,600 people who had been participating in the study for 25 years.

What the researchers discovered was, first-and-foremost, is that people who exercised were definitely living longer than those who do not exercise. This was not a very surprising conclusion. But when researchers deep-dived into the data, they were surprised by what they discovered as it related to the benefits of the different types of exercises the study participants were partaking in.

Cyclists and runners were adding an extra 3.7 and 3.2 years to their lives respectively. But tennis and badminton players were adding an additional 9.7 and 6.2 respective years to their lifespans. Soccer players were adding nearly five years to their lives. Note that tennis and badminton are racquet sports, and are categorized like soccer to be team sports, while cycling and running are characterized by the researchers to be solo or individual sports.

The researchers considered and then generally discounted socioeconomic factors, e.g. people of greater affluence and income have more time to play a racquet sport and would therefore likely live a healthier lifestyle too. The

189

social aspects of the racquet sports were believed by the researchers to be the primary differentiating factor in the advantage between the different sports, not even the physical benefits each sport provided. As one researcher was quoted in saying: "Raising your heart rate is important. But it looks like the connecting with other people is, too."

I would offer that replacing a racquet with a sword places fencing in the same category of team sports as tennis and badminton. From one perspective, these sports can seem like individual sports because there is typically only one person on either side of the net or dividing line. And in this book, I have – correctly in my viewpoint – talked about fencing as a one-on-one combat sport. I have no doubt that anyone watching a competitive tennis match would view those professionals as being in anything but a one-on-one competitive competition. Yet the researchers in the study I have cited here consider tennis and badminton to be a team sport, so it follows that fencing would be included in the team sport category. (Simply swap the racquet for a sword, and there you have it.) Inasmuch as fencing is about the individual as it is in a racquet sport, it is – just like in a racquet sport – about one person competing against another person. And in fencing, badminton, and tennis, sometimes it is about team competition. While there is never more than one person on each side of the fencing piste (strip) at the same time, unlike tennis or badminton where multiple team members can be on their side the court simultaneously, team sport competitions nonetheless require each team member to work with and coordinate with their team members competitively differently than if they were out there by themselves as a team of one.

I understand the researcher's categorization of the identified sports as being team or individual. Even when played as individuals, tennis, badminton, and fencing are competed in social settings. There are other people around. You are competing against another person. Even if you despise your opponent, chances are very good that there are other people in close proximity that you are friendly with. Fencing is often competed in as a team sport, notably at the club and collegiate levels. If you lose your bout or match, you can find a consoling shoulder. You can share the thrill of triumph with your colleagues. There is the opportunity to chat about different topics, just like we do at my fencing club.

Lesson Learned

I do, however, think it is wrong to insinuate that people who enjoy jogging or cycling are some kinds of hermits or isolationists. The fact is that I have enjoyed participation in both of those sports at one time in my life. I appreciated just getting out there and having the time to let my mind drift and see sights I wouldn't normally have a chance to look at when I was driving. (I was also a soccer and racquetball player in my youth.) Plus, lots of people who jog do so these days while listening to their favorite songs or an audiobook, and many cyclists do so in groups or packs. Maybe some people choose some sports out of convenience. Sometimes, it is just nice to separate from the cacophony of life, and some sports permit this.

What about people like me who have participated in both categories of sports identified in the research study? Is there a benefit to having done this? I have discussed in this book the mindset of a fencer and a leader: could it be that sports like tennis, badminton, and fencing which are solo yet social sports provide more benefit than strictly individual sports like jogging and cycling and even have advantages over group sports like soccer? If anyone reading this book is a researcher in the field of sports or health, I think I just provided an outline of a new study for you!

I have showcased the real relationships between fencing strategies and tactics to business throughout this book. It is my opinion that if the research study I mentioned here shows anything, it is that there is also a bit of fencing's individual participant within its social culture that is applicable to today's modern business environment. Dumas's Musketeer creed is an obvious embodiment of the type of team environment that companies should be building and that organizations should be fostering to ensure they are ready to take on the internal issues and external challenges which threaten the ability of the business to execute better each and every day. There could be no better fencing lesson to end this book on than that one.

Let's Review: Masks Off, Weapons Down

Congratulations! You have successfully made it through all of your lessons! So, how do you feel? Wiser? More learned? Ready to face the competition?

In this book, I exposed some common business challenges, posed some key questions that should have made you stop and think, and provided some keen insights to lead you down paths to solutions. It was an enjoyable exercise to do so in combining my love of fencing with my passion for my business profession. The parallels between the sport of fencing and the battles in business are evident as I described in this book. Now, I hope my viewpoints can be of benefit to you in your professional careers and personal efforts.

But as with any sport, or as with anything we endeavor, continued practice will make us proficient as we are unlikely to be experts at the outset. As such, you might very well still need a coach to help you continue your training, guide you, advise you, and correct some mistakes along the way. Don't worry, I am here to help.

If you are interested in the sport of fencing, would like to learn more and give it a try, and live nearby, go to www.tropicalknightsfencing.com and contact me. Even if you are just passing through the area and would like to stop in, or stop by and practice or say hello, that would be just fine.

If your business is struggling for success and needs some help to execute better, please contact me at www.attackparryriposte.com. We'll have a chat and I will let you know how I can help you to defeat the forces foiling your plans and slash through the disruptions causing chaos and are obstacles in the way of your success.

Thank you for your attention and completing your lessons. Put what you have learned into practice and use the knowledge to help your business execute better and become a more successful organization. Just remember to always be en garde for the next challenger ahead. Depending upon factors such as distance and speed and calibration – yours and your opponent's – that next competitor to the achievement of your goals and objectives may be much closer and more threatening than you think.

… Coach Norman, your 'Principal Execution Officer.'